TRIBES OF THE MOON

A Book of Otherkin Coventry, Seasonal Rituals and Lunar Magick for All 13 Moons

Lotuswulf Satyrhorn

authorHOUSE®

AuthorHouse™ LLC
1663 Liberty Drive
Bloomington, IN 47403
www.authorhouse.com
Phone: 1-800-839-8640

Published by AuthorHouse   06/27/2014

ISBN: 978-1-4969-2234-2 (sc)
ISBN: 978-1-4969-2233-5 (e)

Contents

Introduction

The Otherkin community has long been in need of a book such as this. While there are many books of seasonal rituals and guidance for the general Wiccan, witch, pagan, or shaman, and various traditions among them, no one has written a book for the Otherkin with a coven or lunar and seasonal rites in mind. To write such a book requires it to come from a long-term, serious practitioner of the Otherkin persuasion. Since this is written from a highly eclectic point of view, the rituals herein are available to everyone, Otherkin or not. But it is intended for those who wish to start an Otherkin coven, be a part of and lead rituals with other "*kin*" and raise the magick of their life and the Earth to a higher state of being. This book will also be helpful to those who are considering or are already adding a member to their coven that claims the Otherkin path. While I realize that not all "*kin*" will be apt to join a coven or practice the magical arts, this book is for those that do or are looking for a way to present themselves to the surrounding magical and pagan community.

The path of the Otherkin is difficult enough, trying to manage with animal feelings and connections, phantom parts and wild urges, while being trapped in a world full of "*humans*" that have no understanding of the underlying depth and spiritual magick of the Otherkin spirit. The Otherkin persona tends to have a lack of structure for the religious aspects and getting organized, and in this lack, we suffer. I present the Otherkin path here as a spiritual practice and way of life rather than a religion. If we use spiritual techniques from various traditions to give us spiritual and magical experiences in life, we can be rid of the need for a religious basis, aside from *"practicing it religiously."* It is in the purpose of this book to present the Otherkin path as shamanic sorcery and witchcraft, and as a *"tradition"* which can stand on its own, eclectic and free, breaking the rules of what witch's covens are being turned into. From the Otherkin perspective, and I can't speak for us all, covens should be about practicing magick and healing each other, rather than gathering like some tired old church goers, going through the motions expected of us, to worship something deemed greater than ourselves. I know much of the pagan community will claim to *"stand by the gods"* but in the *"worship of"* they tend to lose sight of the true purpose. While children may idolize their parents until they grow up, they must then learn to emulate them in the proper context and with their own wisdom, thereby living their own life. By this I mean that we may be able to rise to become as the forest spirits and *"gods"* in our own afterlife, for the next generations of magical practitioners and Otherkin. There is a similar belief in the Shinto tradition of Japan. Many of the priests of Shinto, want to become and believe in the possibility of becoming *"kami"* i.e. nature spirits, in their afterlife vision. This easily translates to the Otherkin, believing in our true selves as being connected and related to various animals and nature spirits. This is the reason for leaving behind the conventional ideas of Coventry, to raise ourselves up together and realize, that that which we call divine, is the inner spirit of every creature on the Earth today. In this enlightened realization we see the truth, not to worship anything, but to work with, the moon phases and Earth's seasonal changes, to achieve our goals and be as an aid in changing the future of mankind. May we walk forth in strength and harmony, and claim our path as Otherkin.

May you be blessed
upon your path!

Lotuswulf Satyrhorn

Chapter One
Otherkin Coventry

To re-envision the long-standing ideas of a witch's coven is a difficult task. The Otherkin coven has to be able to break through the boundaries of what is accepted by the magical community at large and create something that appeals to a broad audience for spiritual practices without losing its individual, Otherkin nature. In this daunting task, we must look at the ideas of the witch's coven as a *"religious"* group, and remove the social stigma from the rest of society. In keeping with the Otherkin spiritual aspect, we have to be able to have organization without dogma, protect against competition among the members, and have a *"priesthood"* that act as guides and teachers, rather than *"religious leaders."*

It would seem senseless to finally throw off the chains of mainstream religion, only to become weighted down by the excessive rules of another. My vision of an Otherkin coven is one of community and acceptance, as well as a place of spiritual and magical learning, encouragement and deeply earth based spirituality. The word *"coven"* comes from the word, *"covenant"* which means, *"a binding agreement made by two or more individuals."* In this *"binding agreement"* the Otherkin accepts a path of spiritual practice and agrees to take part in rites and practices that embrace spiritual freedom for each individual and grants equal right to the whole. This means that the spiritual law of respect and responsibility is the main key to the binding agreement of the Otherkin coven.

I realize that the true meaning of the word, *"Coventry"* is defined as, *"ostracized, or refuse to speak to,"* and in its irony of applying this word to a witch's coven, we are ostracized for our varying belief by the mainstream of society, as well as misunderstood by those who are close relation, i.e. witches. It is from our binding agreement in the coven and social ostracization that we must ask the following question.

Gathering the Tribe – Are Witches Otherkin?

When we set out to find members and assemble a coven of Otherkin, we will undoubtedly run into young witches that are interested in joining a coven, but at the mention of Otherkin, they may change their mind. If we tell them that the coven for Otherkin is based in shamanic witchcraft and is very eclectic in its approach, they might reconsider. So we ask the question, are witches Otherkin?

We can argue this point for a long time and unless the right information is made available the disagreement will remain at a standstill. In order to succeed in clarifying this debate, we have to define both, what the Otherkin really are, and what makes a shamanic witch. Otherkin can be defined as a group of people that believe in themselves to be spiritually related to and identified with, something *"Other"* than human. It is in the mind's identification with an animal spirit or the spirit of a mythical creature that truly defines the Otherkin experience. Now let us consider the word *"human"* from this perspective, and we end up with the thoughts of, *"non-magical beings, with a lack of wisdom and spiritual drive, that refuse to see the interconnectedness of life on Earth."* Now from that perspective, the word, *"witch"* could be described as, *"a follower or practitioner of an ancient pagan religion, relating to early man and tribal healing; sorcery, a practitioner of magic, and a person who relates to the term witch as a part of their identification with an Earth based religion."* (No, these are not in the dictionary, but I take from what society might describe.) So, with this information in place, do we call a witch, Otherkin? In a way they are, and if they advance in the craft as totemists, spiritual shapeshifter's, shamanic practitioners, or as the magical sorcerer/ess, then my answer is yes, they can fit into the Otherkin persona and be a member of the tribe of Otherkin. I started out in Wicca, some nineteen years ago, and in realizing that Wicca had become a waste of time, I began really seeking spiritual advancement. It is in the advanced practices that the witch turns into a shaman, which in turn can find the inter-relation with beings from the animal kingdom and mythical realms, which are the home of our Otherkin spirit. It is well known that shamans often consider themselves related to various animals through totems, power animals, etc, and in a way that connects them to Otherkin. So, in the case of witches being Otherkin, the question is not are they considered Otherkin, but do they want to advance to become an Otherkin, finding their inner spiritual self with the coven and engaging in shamanic journey practices, healing, sorcery, etc.

Another difficulty in creating an Otherkin coven is the many varying aspects of the Otherkin persona. Trying to write and create ritual workings for a group with differing aspects such as dragons, vampires, fae-folk, satyrs, wolves, mer-folk and others can pose a challenge, especially for the newly gathered tribe. The point to realize is that each member can be a part of the ritual writing in respect to their own "*liturgy*" or the group can concentrate on the purpose of the rite, rather than the individual kin amongst the coven. It raises the ideal of, "*we are all classified as Otherkin*," that we gather together to honor the cycles of the Moon, or the Earth, or celebrate the turn of the seasons. It becomes a celebration of the differences, working together and honoring each other in the coven setting.

Setting Goals & Rules

It seems obvious to most that if we are going to create any group of people working together for a common goal, we need to set those goals clearly and put together a set of rules to follow within the coven setting. This is actually another problem found when creating an Otherkin coven. Otherkin tend to stand outside the social structure and too many rules are completely pointless for us. I was once given the impression of a list of rules from a local Wiccan based coven that was starting to sound like a new law book, or the Bill of Rights, with phrases similar to, *"clause A part B states that ..."* I refuse to join anything that starts off that way.

When setting rules for an Otherkin coven, keep to the point of respect and responsibility, as this will show greater wisdom in the long run for the group. Stating simple things like, *"Show up on time or call ahead if running late for meetings"* and *"give respect to all members,"* is fair to all involved and shows you who among the group really takes it seriously. Instead of holding some *"coven court meeting"* when trouble arises to decide if the member will be *"excommunicated,"* simply ask them what the problem is and if they want to continue their membership in the group. They may have family difficulties that they don't want to speak about, or any number of things that concern them which need to be addressed and maybe even brought to light in front of the group, to consider the covens ability to help them heal past the problem, if they so choose. Communication is key in any relationship, beit with your family, spouse, children, or "Other."

For the newly formed coven, setting goals for the group to achieve should be according to spans of time that the coven remains together. What are the coven's goals for the next six months, or a year? Do you want more members or to learn more about a particular subject? What about a comfortable meeting place where an altar or other such tools can be left available? Do you want to add new or more practices to the group? Ask among members for ideas on what they want to focus on, as well as what may be needed for ritual workings or adding new tools to work with. If a new coven is created and approached with the proper mindframe, the practices and studies can be shared among members as well as making a group with a strong bond to each other, and this may be the most important aspect of the coven gathering. Teach openness and community, as well as wisdom, and the light will shine for the coven no matter how dark times may get.

Selecting a Priest/ess – Guide to Group Work

Finding a long-term member of the Otherkin path, to act as a guide to the coven, might be one of the hardest tasks for the newly formed group to overcome. It would make sense that the practitioner with the most experience would be the priest or priestess of the coven, but may not always be the case. Abilities and desire to teach others, patience, compassion and people skills as well as general knowledge of the work should be considered. Some might say that the founding member of the coven is the leader, but this may be a case of an individual's desire to be a part of a group, to learn from and with others. Some people, Otherkin or not are talented at attracting people without trying, while others tend to stray from the center of attention and stay in the shadows so to speak. If a coven has members of varying degrees in magical and healing skills, it may be best to allow each member to work with the others within their skill level. In this way, each member can contribute and help in teaching the others about things that they are good at, giving demonstrations or performing certain rites, spells or healings, without having to appoint one particular leader for the group.

This gives each member of the group a place to start from and then add to their own knowledge by listening to others creating a fellowship of the coven. Having a feeling of belonging and importance for what each individual can bring to the coven can help in further strengthening the bonds of the membership. This type of tactic will be a great asset to those covens who utilize it and work together to teach new members, share stories and experiences, as well as teaching and learning from each other. Just remember that each person learns in their own way and time and if they need to get a different example or technique from another practitioner or member of the coven to not take the matter personally, but encourage the ability of each Otherkin coven member. All Otherkin must keep in mind that we can learn more from each other about different experiences, opinions and techniques and create a deeper life experience for ourselves, and each other.

Priesthood – Teaching Among the Ranks

For the coven that has or creates an assigned priesthood, the priest and/or priestess that lead the group need to be highly aware and advanced in their craft and as individuals. It should be preferred that they are certified in a few different healing modalities, shamanic practices and well knowledged in herb and spellcraft, and be at least a ten to fifteen (+) year practitioner. I state a requirement like this because if we allow someone to take charge that isn't ready for such a role, it can end in disaster for the coven and possibly give rise to an ego/

power trip for the coven leader(s). The other reasoning for such a well-trained individual is that in the case of some shamanic-based rituals, such as shapeshifting rites, many things have a possibility to go awry, and this can end in a bad press episode for the coven as well as the Otherkin in general. Even trained priests should approach Shapeshifting rituals with caution, as we are essentially playing with what modern society would call madness. We cannot always know who has the capability to go beyond the ordinary world and come back safely and sanely. If your priesthood is weak, they will either try to cover the experience, leaving a person stuck in a bad and potentially dangerous mindframe, or simply remove the person from the coven. A trained priest will do their best to help the individual heal and come back to normal consciousness.

When working with an organized priesthood, we should be able to reach for our very best inner self, in a safe environment. This should be the person we trust most in the coven setting and are able to speak to them with an open heart and mind, and know that they will do the same for us. Being a teacher of spiritual practices takes a lot of years of knowledge, personal experience and a well-tuned intuition to be as a guide for members of an Otherkin coven.

Coven Meditation Practices

The practice of meditation should be first and foremost in the creation of the Otherkin coven. My reasoning behind this is simple. Meditation clears the mind and aids in removing the emotional and mental baggage that are a direct result of life in the modern era. Meditation also helps in focusing the mind for various magical practices and healing work. If a group of people begin with practicing meditation together, again sharing in experiences, difficulties, and techniques outside of or after each meditation session, the group is more likely to attain a stronger foundation for long-term membership, as well as a sense of bonding with each other that will last a lifetime. For those among the coven that practice meditations, different techniques can be shared and taught to each other at different intervals. Research for meditation classes and techniques can be attained simply on the Internet these days and each member can be given a print out to take with them to practice on their own and within the coven.

When learning meditation, begin with the simplest practice (Zen) of counting the breathing cycles, from one to ten, then start over. By focusing on the breath, we give the mind something to focus on, while clearing away the unnecessary thoughts and feelings that will arise. When the mind becomes distracted, following other thoughts or feelings, bring the attention back to the breath and return to your counting practice without judging the self for losing focus or concentration. It is the creation of a silent mind from between the thoughts, that slowly pushes away the constant mental chatter and gives the practitioner a feeling of clarity in life's many difficult situations.

For group meditations, chanting mantras, practicing visualizations, kundalini yoga, qigong and many other techniques can be used to spiritually empower and teach each member of the coven. Creating mantras for the Otherkin experience, along with spellcraft to further the work, can be a great aid in the art of Otherkin spirituality. (For more information on creating Otherkin mantras and meditations, see the author's first work, *"The Book of Satyr Magick."*)

The practice of meditation, along with other techniques, eventually creates a clear mind that is not impeded with worries and concerns and allows the practitioner to find the inner peace taught by and sought after, within many different magical and spiritual traditions. This clear state of mind and being allows the practitioner to channel more energy for healing and magic, gain access to transcendental planes and experiences, and to attain a greater sense of wisdom and peace from within.

Notes on "Contradictory Spirits" & Creating Harmony in the Coven

Among our society, and indeed our lives, we will eventually meet someone that seems to be our polar opposite. This is the person that undermines our efforts or causes us problems from the beginning. In a spiritual sense, this may mean that the spirits and energies that we work with and keep around us are contradictory or opposed to the energies that another person holds around them. Whether we see this energy as predator and prey animals, or spirits that just don't like each other, the issue remains no matter how we view it. This meeting of contradictory spirits will cause excessive drama and a falling apart of the coven, if not controlled or removed. Herein lies the tough question of what to do about conflicting personalities. At times it may be clear that one person, especially on an energetic level, may feel in some way either threatened by or think they are superior to the other, depending on what the underlying issue really is. If such a problem occurs in a coven setting, it will be of utmost importance to seat both individuals and ask them first if they really wish to continue with the group work. If they had no problems prior to their meeting, then this can be an issue that can be resolved if both people wish it. This can be a matter of energy and acceptance of inner aspects that are at the time denied. If you have a wise priesthood, or someone with some counseling training, they should be able to resolve the issue peacefully if both parties will comply and communicate. I have met a few individuals in my own life that at first meeting, we did not like each other. As we spent time around each other in school, we learned that we were actually very similar in attitudes and personality, even agreeing on the same music. It wasn't long before we became close friends for a number of years.

I realize that the *"normal"* person will end up causing more drama by trying to make one individual in the situation leave automatically. An action such as removing one person may cause friends of that person to act out or leave as well. This is a Christianized tactic and not a very wise one to use, as it shows automatic judgment, rather than true understanding. It is popular among groups to just remove one person and yet they fail the spiritual challenge if they fall into this trap. Covens are not created to play political roles or to control what people do and with whom. They are intended to encourage the spiritual growth of each member and if the members need to seek other avenues for growth, then so be it. In the process of spiritual growth and understanding the self, we must learn to understand the energies at play within our own lives and that these same energies are at play in the lives of all other people. It is this realization that we are able to find a place of harmony within us and in the world around us.

Now I know that there are times when someone needs to be removed from a situation that is not beneficial to them or the people around them. But if we are going to claim spiritual wisdom, we need to be in a place in our mind and heart to try to use it first, before resulting to judgmental actions that have been used against us. (Burn the witch rather than listen to what they have to say!)

Creating a harmonious coven is a challenge, as people are apt to reach for drama rather than wisdom when in a group situation. You could add that to the rules if you wanted as, *"no excessive drama"* but would people understand it? The truth is that life has enough drama without adding insult to injury. Whether the drama of birth, death, the beginning of school, graduating from school or college, relationships, vacations, all things are a form of drama. Even living alone and not relating to society, is a type of depressing drama. Harmony doesn't mean that we only do things that are peaceful or in a peaceful manner, as then we lose energy. Nor does it mean that we only listen to certain *"calming"* types of music, as we need rhythm to survive and thrive. Harmony is created when we focus on what we are doing, and put our heart into it. This includes all the people involved in the coven of the Otherkin.

Gathering for "Needed Magick"
Abundance & Prosperity for the Coven

The magic of *"need"* can be some of the most powerful magic worked. My terminology here comes from the knowing that, often times, the *"needs"* of individual members of a coven are overlooked or left up to the individual to resolve. Here again is the idea that covens should gather for magic and healing rather than only for religious observance. In this work of *"needed magic,"* the coven is gathered to work rites and spells of prosperity and wealth for the whole of the coven. This requires the energy of all members and to ensure that each member is well taught in their craft and participating in the spell or ritual. In this way, we can create abundance and growth for the whole of the coven rather than a few members being *"well-off"* financially, while the rest can barely make it through the week. It is understandable that not everyone will be able to achieve success or financial gain at the same time and an understanding amongst the coven of the rules of *"money magic,"* is important.

For the basics of money magic, understand that the universe cannot create from nothing, but has to bring about change in the way that works best for each individual. This means that, in working spells for more money, it may create a situation of job loss, to find a better position, give a chance for a raise, or create more hours for overtime pay. This depends upon the current financial position and the *"realm of possibilities"* of the person. Working in our *"realm of possibilities"* can be frustrating. For those who are new to this subject, the *"realm of possibilities"* is the area(s) of life that you have been trained in or are capable to use for your growth. In other words, if you have a college degree in one or more area(s), you cannot apply that to a different area(s) without going back to school, to make additions to your realm of ability. So if you have a job already, you have a greater realm of possibilities than someone who does not but you are still limited by your possibilities, through a pay raise or change in position within the company. In a way, the jobless person has more possibilities if they are intelligent and capable of more than a few different types of work or lifestyle. This is the path of a shapeshifter, or a being that can adapt to many different ways of life and remain true to their inner self throughout. Trying to create a change where there is a seeming lack of possibility puts a wall between us and the financial gain and independence that we seek. If we consider the way in which some *"well-off"* or *"rich"* people have attained this, it is by having a variety of different capabilities and using them to the fullest extent, in order to make money. This is a truth that may be hard to swallow.

Another aspect of money magic requires healing work for the chakras, while paying close attention to the state of mind. There are times in which, we as individuals don't realize that we have been taught something different about money, or hold a mental attitude towards it, that keeps us from attaining any real growth or financial change in our lives. Those of us that come from *"humble beginnings"* know that money has been a problem in our life and until we realize and face our fears, we cannot move forward. Holding on to attitudes such as *"money is the enemy,"* or that we *"aren't good enough"* or a fear of success (or failure) will stand in the way of changing our financial position. Like it or not, these attitudes and suppressed feelings about money are held in the chakras and will arise as an imbalance within them. This is often but not always held in the sacral chakra or our seat of abundance and self-worth. I know that most will relate the sacral chakra to sexual energy and creativity, but this is also our own ability to nurture ourselves and gain independence. The *"Emperor or Empress"* is the positive archetype of this area of the chakra centers, being able to create abundance for self and family, while the negative archetype is the Martyr, or archetype of self-sacrifice. A practice of healing this chakra and creating an affirmation of the ability to attain success and the self worth to go along with it can alleviate the problem in time.

The main idea behind this section of needed magic is that an individual or coven can't grow if the members are constantly in a state of financial distress. The point here again is that if we work together in a coven setting to teach and learn about the many difficulties we all share in life, then we can have the opportunity to create change in the world around us. A coven, no matter how strong of a bond, will fall if financial problems plague the group. I know that witches, Otherkin and most metaphysical practitioners are often challenged in the world of money, as we often see it as destructive to the self and soul path. But money plays a part in everything in society, from stopping animal abuse to saving the rainforest. Money also gives free time to work on spiritual practices, reading new books or finding and buying tools for the various practices we enjoy as Otherkin. We may as well raise our selves up and attain mastery of the world of money, on the road to spiritual wisdom and freedom. (For more information and a money ritual, check chapter 6.)

Honoring Each Others Totems & Spirits

One of the most important rituals for a coven of Otherkin is a ritual of honoring each other's totems and inner Otherkin spirits. This rite is a statement made by each member in turn of acknowledging the spiritual aspects of all the other members in the coven. This is simple and yet profound, as we create a sense of community in honor, and recognition of the inner soul or spirit self among each member of the group. This recognition of spirit and honor, acts, as in many other things, to create a ripple effect outwards to other aspects of life. The act of a simple Ceremony of Honor at the beginning of the coven meetings will raise much energy and morale for the group, increasing the chances of success for a long-term coven. It also requires each member of the coven to know each other's totems or inner spirits, at least to some degree. The only trick here is that each member be sincere in their respect and honor to each other.

In understanding a Ritual of Honor amongst Kin, we need to look at the rituals of most all pagan-based religions. These are rites of honor, devotion and sincerity directed at the gods of the people. This is not to say that we *"worship"* these people, but that we honor the divine aspect or spirit within that person or group of people. In Rites of the Moon, we honor the Moon as our spiritual mother, grandmother or sister in some respects, asking for guidance, psychic ability, strength, power, etc. In Rites for the Earth, we honor the Earth Mother's abundance and ask that it touch our lives that we may prosper as well. In honoring the totems of an individual, we can attain some of the ability of that totem, develop a better understanding of the person and totem, whether or not it is active in our life, and begin to learn the true spiritual insight of an enlightened master. This practice will eventually help us to *"see"* the spiritual Otherkin aspects of other people in our life and recognize different totems amongst crowds of individuals. This could also have farther- reaching effects, as we change our view of each other, we change our view of other people. This could slowly eliminate some of the degradation of all people and the objectification of women.

A rite or Ceremony of Honor doesn't have to be long-winded or excessive with garnishments. It is about each member of the coven taking a moment to look into the eyes of each other member, bowing while holding the hands/fists out in a prayer pose or one fist in the other open hand and saying something simple like:

I honor the spirit/totem(s) of _____ within you. I give you respect as the spirit in form.

Now the practitioner shakes the hand of the member they are facing, or a half sided hug amongst a brother/ sisterhood then moves to the next person, and repeats. As each member of the coven finishes the ceremony, they stop at the end of the line, and the next person will begin with whom ever is standing next to them and so on and so forth. Let each of the members give their honor and then proceed with whatever the coven gathering is about. This ceremony is based in Buddhism and the idea of honoring the Buddha nature in each and every person, as we can all attain to greatness if we but realize our true spiritual self. A ritual such as this one may help to contain the drama we spoke about earlier, as it is difficult to look someone in the eye and honor their spirit or totems and stay angry, jealous, etc, of them in some way. Practice respect and sincerity with this ritual, as you will.

Crafting Tools for Magick

In an Otherkin coven, it will be important to be able to craft as many of your own tools as possible, but keep in mind that the most important tool that any witch or Otherkin has is a strong mind and belief in them selves. Crafting your own tools is also intensely satisfying and benefits your growth on the path. Among the many tools of magick, they are all intended to be as an extension of the self in the physical world, to channel spiritual energy for whatever ritual or spell is being worked. When we craft our own tools, we place a lot of our own energy into them, so when crafting, keep your mind focused on the task and you will craft a piece that extends and directs your energy with ease.

I know that there are enough magical and spiritual crafters in the world and it is easier to just put the money together and buy them. Some tools such as a hammer or axe, will have to be bought, but each member of the group can add and adorn as they feel is right for their Otherkin spirit. In a way, buying too many tools takes from your ability to decide, following spirit guidance, in what the particular item should be and/or look like. Just because it doesn't have a battery pack or flashing lights and looks more than rustic, doesn't mean it won't work. It is about the natural aspect and staying away from too many machines to do the work. A simple wand can be more effective than one that has been made by machinery. Sure they are pretty, but this is a path of breaking the ego, and pretty isn't always the best choice. If we think about the way that true witches from long ago really did things, each witch that joined a coven either made their own tools or the tools were given to them as gifts from the members of the coven. If an Otherkin coven wants to follow something like this as a part of their tradition, simple hand tools are very effective with a little practice and search the forests, rivers, lakes and fields for the items you will use for your magical tools. Items found in natural settings can make all of your staffs, wands, walking sticks, a thyrsus, and rattles, and will keep with honoring the spirits that we work with.

After you have crafted your magical tools, be sure to charge them under the full or new moons so as to create an even deeper bond between the practitioner and the item that has been made.

Using A Coven Medicine Shield

For the totemist aspect of the Otherkin spirit, a medicine shield can be a good representation of the energy of the gathering tribe. Deciding to use a medicine shield for gatherings gives all members an image and energy to honor within themselves. A coven medicine shield doesn't have to be a store bought depiction of one animal either. Some native shields are just a piece of fur tied to the hoop, while others can be stretched leather painted into the desired symbolism of the group. This does require some work and crafting on the part of the coven members but working together is a major point for the coven anyway.

I realize that most medicine shields that are available for purchase today are only four or five different animals. The commonly seen shield is either a wolf, bear, eagle, cougar or deer, with an occasional elk or owl and all of these animals have great qualities for leadership and teaching spiritual knowledge but may not work for your individual needs. Purchasing your own tanned leather, leather straps and hoops from a local craft store can be a way to create your own coven medicine shield and get the design on it that best symbolizes your group. This leather once stretched with leather straps and tied to the hoop, can be painted or adorned with feathers and beads as the group see fit, using stencils or pre-drawing the image with a pencil before committing it to paint or ink. Create a hanger on the top of the hoop with leather straps and place in your meeting area as a reminder of the reason and energy for the group. Tribal imagery can aid in changing the mindframe of the people gathered to focus on the purpose rather than letting idol chatter take away from the group's workings.

The group members should also charge a medicine shield for the coven for whatever purpose the imagery serves. Using magic as we craft our tools and ritually charging them to be an extension of our energy is just as important as having the imagery to aid in altering the mind. Use the medicine shield for gatherings and remind each member to honor the spirit energy when gathered for coven workings.

Initiation Rites

When adding new members to a coven, the rites of initiation are deemed very important. Usually the initiate is intended to undergo certain training prior to the initiation rituals, but often times, in modern covens the training is somehow overlooked. The word *initiate*, has two important definitions for this in Webster's New World Dictionary as, 1. *"to bring into practice or use,"* and 2. *"to teach the fundamentals of some subject to."* This means that an initiation rite should be performed to show the new members' skill level and willingness to use the information attained. The ritual for initiation is therefore, similar to a rite of passage, to recognize an attainment of knowledge, power, etc., and in the ritual of initiation, the new member is putting this knowledge to use. Often times, modern initiations are simply performed as an acceptance of the new member by the group, through questioning etc., without any real training required. This can also be the problem for new covens and the fact that many, donot last beyond a year or two, due to lack of any real spiritual or magical knowledge among the members. This lack of knowledge among the groups that call themselves a *"witch's coven,"* is the reason that many people leave witchcraft and spirituality behind in favor of weak mainstream religions. If they aren't being taught anything real and being given a spiritual experience to verify it, then it just becomes the mumbo-jumbo of superstition. It is in this that witchcraft and Otherkin practices don't grow any larger in number and seems to actually lose more members than it keeps.

In shamanic spiritual practices, the spirits that guide the shaman are most often the creators and instigators of the shamanic initiation experience. This is the push from the spirit realm that makes the shaman heal him or herself, thus, being initiated by a very difficult experience. While this goes against what much of society agrees with, it is in our most difficult of times that we will rise to attain spiritual knowledge and power or simply die. The Otherkin coven cannot force its initiates to undergo such straining circumstances and expect to have very many in number. So where do we draw the line between physical initiation rites and letting the spirits teach the newcomer? The answer is in undergoing spiritual ordeals for the initiation ritual.

Before pushing someone into an ordeal ritual, begin with teaching them information about the rite, the what's, why's, where's and how's. Give them an understanding of what they need to do or accomplish through the use of the ritual. Take time to teach them techniques for meditation and be sure that they have a good grasp of the information and ability with it, before setting them off to the ordeal initiation. If a person has issues with anxiety or panic attacks, breathing trouble, blood pressure problems, etc., don't force them to go through an ordeal that may cause them to develop those symptoms into a life-threatening situation. Again a well-trained priesthood is required for teaching and guiding through an ordeal rite for initiation.

Ordeals can be used for many varying aspects of initiations. From beginning shapeshifting techniques to learning a particular technique for healing, the initiation is the testing period after learning the information and practicing with it. This can be practiced on their own, in a group, and/or with someone standing-by for guidance as needed. The point is to ensure that the initiate is trained prior to achieving the initiation ritual. The initiatory path of infernal traditions is encouraged for the Otherkin coven members, as this is the path of being initiated over many times, in many ways throughout this lifetime, to attain a greater spiritual state of being before the death of this body. This period of training also serves to ensure that the initiate is truly ready for the rite and comfortable in their knowledge and practice before being pushed into the ritual, not knowing what is expected, needed, etc. In shamanic spiritual traditions, it is often said that the spirits (or God, in some cases,) won't give you something that you aren't ready for. The same should hold true for the ordeal rites of the Otherkin coven.

Ordeal rituals can take on many forms for different things and can be used from the milder of initiations to the most extreme. The following list is for initiation ordeals and will range from the mild to the more extreme, but in most cases will be safe with the use of common sense and intelligence.

Naked & Alone – teaches awareness of self and surroundings and how to connect with primal energy of survival, connection with the inner animal(s)

Cleansing Sweat – aids cleansing the body of toxins, for purification on the path, teaches understanding of heat and endurance

Biting Cold – teaches endurance against the harshness of winter, earth and water elements, forces use of deep breathing techniques in order to warm the self, survival and willpower

Keeper of the Flame – teaches discipline and gives time to contemplate the ways the fire element influences life, understanding of fire and its positive use, endurance and illumination of the spirit

Flogging Rites – teaches shapeshifting through controlled pain, release of endorphins and adrenaline, raises kundalini for shifting experience

Vampiric Death Ordeal – most difficult ordeal for removing negative aspects of the self, mysteries of life and death, rebirth to the new aspects

Ceremony of the Black Flame – teaches separation from society in order to understand the self, following the inner spirit, breaks ego tendencies, destroys church's influences, fears & rules.

So, here is my list of seven different ordeal styled rites that are written out in detail in my first book, "*The Book of Satyr Magick.*" These are easily used as initiation rites for the coven setting and will require training before sending the new initiate into the ordeal. Use common sense in any ordeal rite and the initiate will attain a new sense of confidence and growth within the Otherkin coven.

Healing & Empowerment Rites

The path of the Otherkin requires much in the ways of healing and spiritual empowerment. To truly attain a deeper state of mind and soul, we must heal the aspects of self that keep us from our goals, thereby turning ignorance into understanding and weakness into strength. The practices of healing and empowerment of the self and spirit amongst the Otherkin coven should be of prime importance to all members. The practice of gathering for healing work and empowerment rituals should take precedence over the common chatter amongst people, as this simple discipline itself is empowerment. In a coven setting, it can be difficult to admit when we feel like we need some sort of healing work, beit through chakra balancing or Reiki, or a balancing of the elements through trance states, drumming, dance and chanting. Empowerment is a major key to this spiritual path and is to be embraced by all coven members. I realize that many authors of "*infernal traditions*" tend to leave out anything on healing the self and being in balance. But if you are going to reap the benefits of shapeshifting rites or lunar ceremonies, you need to be as balanced as possible before beginning so as to attain as much as possible from the rituals that you work with. Being in balance and finding a state of harmony is the purpose to virtually all spiritual traditions, whether Otherkin, Satanism, shamanic, pagan, Buddhist, etc. These various traditions, if true to spiritual growth, want their members to achieve a state of enlightenment and an understanding of the universe that we reside in. Healing and empowerment rites may be the key to unlocking the doors for your individual Otherkin experience.

For coven healing rites, set up a practice of performing rituals of healing a day or two prior to lunar workings, so as to utilize the lunar energy of the growing/waxing moon for opening the chakras of each member. Cleansing rites can be performed before new moon rituals to clear away debris that gets stuck in the aura. If you have very many quartz crystals available among the coven, these can be cleansed and used in a crystal grid for healing during the group's meditation sessions. Sound healing can also be an option during meditations so as to increase the spiritual vibrations of the session and aid in aligning the chakras of those present. For other empowerment work, take the coven on a field trip, hiking in the forest, bike riding, swimming, etc, as all activities will affect the chakras and empower the practitioners during the trip. Finding ways to empower the group as a whole can be a challenge and yet become very rewarding for all members in the long-term Otherkin coven.

Utilizing the "Other" in Daily Life

The practice of using our magical and spiritual abilities in daily life is an important aspect of all magical practice. For the Otherkin, abilities can range from heightened psychic perceptions or animal instincts to empathy and from clairvoyant dreams to seeing auras. The importance here is that we acknowledge and use the psychic input that we receive in order to know when to influence events or people, and when to be ready for problems to bubble to the surface. So many practitioners teach the use of ritual and spells and never include the use of these inner spiritual and magical abilities in day-to-day life and being. Otherkin covens should take the time to listen to each other when speaking about these abilities and each can again learn new abilities with the practice of working among the group. Some people will have natural abilities that lie dormant until they are recognized or admitted to the self, while others will need to practice accordingly in order to attain these different abilities. The point here is that each of us has ability that we need to incorporate into our daily life, so as to live a more fulfilling existence spiritually. We can help others understand what we experience if we find ways to communicate about it and most all, be honest about what you do or don't perceive or understand.

Another important point to make here is that if one person in the coven doesn't feel that they have psychic abilities, don't patronize or ostracize them for not having your specific ability. Some of us grow into these things as we age in years on the path of spiritual practice. Be patient and let them learn so as to spread the energy of psychic ability farther.

Using and trusting psychic powers seems ridiculous to the normal person. Knowing when to keep what we do to our self and when to share amongst others is very empowering for the individual. Remember the rule of silence when in the company of non-magical people and use your abilities in your life for your fullest advantage.

Practicing Shapeshifting as a Coven

One of the most extreme rituals of the Otherkin coven is that of shapeshifting. These rites are highly personal as they utilize the raising of the kundalini serpent i.e., raw sexual energy, in order to attain the state of consciousness necessary for a shapeshifting experience. Breathing techniques for a group and a little ritually dramatic acting to influence the shift can also be used. For coven shapeshifting rites, it will be necessary to have a circle physically drawn and energetically charged upon the ground or floor of the ritual area. Make sure that it is big enough for the ritual participants to move about and raise energy without stepping or otherwise moving out of the circle. Make an agreement that if a participant steps out of the circle or in a worst-case scenario, tries to *"go after someone,"* that they are to disconnect from the energy of the shift. Remember that these are dangerous rites to work with, especially in a group. Make sure that all involved understand the possibilities and are in sound mind, with no chemical substances such as alcohol or hallucinogens when engaging the shifting experience.

Using hand signals can be a great method of communication between people that are experiencing the shift. A simple *"thumbs up"* *"thumbs down"* or *"ok"* hand signal can be the difference between problems in the ritual and a good experience for all involved. This lets you know if they are *"okay"* or in need of assistance, or just need a moment to allow the energy to dissipate. Don't make the hand signals too complex as trying to communicate can be difficult during the shapeshifting experience, and the use of the voice is almost out of the question.

For the dramatic aspect of the shapeshifting ritual, all the participants should be able to howl, perform low guttural growls and work with intensive *"raging"* breathing, and walk or move about as needed. A crouched position on all fours can be useful as well as a *"circle dance"* which looks similar to a mosh pit, stomping and jumping about in a circle to a drum beat, to raise the animal energy. The shapeshifting experience is very primal and can be intense on the practitioner, if allowed to move with the energy of the shift. This heightened energy must be controlled though, for the sake of the other participants. I hesitated to say *"mosh pit"* as most people think of *"slam-dancing"* but this is not the case. It isn't necessary to slam into each other to bring about the shapeshifting experience, only to move about in a primal manner to raise the kundalini serpent. For those that do not want the shapeshifting ritual to be so active and dramatic, there is another method of helping someone force a shifting experience through what I have created and termed, kundalini massage.

Kundalini massage is a technique that I developed for working with others to give them an experience of shapeshifting without excessive training. This practice works by creating an alternating, rhythmic pattern on the muscle tissue, up the spine to about the shoulder at the base the neck, and returns back down the side to the hip and then again back up the spine. This pattern is alternated between the left and right sides, so that one side is always rising, to increase the energy flow of the kundalini. This type of massage work can become very fast and intense, so a lot of massage oil may be needed. Be careful not to put too much pressure on the muscles along the spinal column, so as to achieve the faster movements and use the thumbs or base of the palm for the center of the back. Unlike regular massage practices, the recipient is encouraged to move as needed, stretching the back and shoulders or moving the arms up above shoulder level during the massage, to increase and engage in the flow of energy. This can work well for an initiation into shapeshifting rituals and with the proper practitioner or priest/ess performing the massage work, will result in a well-controlled shapeshifting experience. The following image gives an example of the movements for those that wish to learn such a practice. **This is not certified by any state regulations for massage practice and is only intended for the metaphysical and spiritual work within this book.**

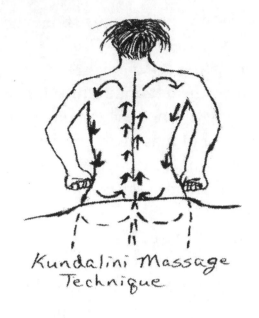

Kundalini Massage
Technique

As you can see from this image, the recipient only needs to be nude or uncovered on the back and at the top of the hips & buttocks, so as to utilize the muscle tissue at the closest point to the base chakra without the requirement of full nudity. The hips will tend to hold a lot of tension and energy, so working into the muscle will aid the release of the kundalini. If you already work with some type of massage techniques, use them and help the recipient relax prior to the ritual working, as relaxed muscles will be more conducive to the shapeshifting experience. At the end of the rite, after the recipient has experienced the shift and perhaps even says a safe word for ending, the masseuse can slow the rhythm and bring the practitioner's energy back to normal, while leaving them energized. This allows the recipient to integrate the shapeshifting energy into his or her own system for use at a later time.

For the purposes of shapeshifting initiation rites, be sure that women are allowed to have other women present during the rite, or a female member of the coven is performing the massage work, so as to feel safe in the group. Don't go through with it if you feel in any way threatened or as if to be putting your life and body in danger. Groups may wish to have one particular trust-worthy member to perform the massage and could train others during the process, so that each recipient comes out of the experience, relaxed and full of energy.

Of course, shapeshifting rites can and should be incorporated into the lunar rites of the coven. Some may choose to only use shifting at certain times of the year, like during the Blood Moon of October or the Wolf Moon of January, while others will practice shifting at most all lunar rites. Shapeshifting experiences can be very empowering for the individual and are suggested for those that wish to truly engage in the Otherkin self. Shapeshifting practices are not by definition only to be used by those who identify as Therian, either. Elves, witches, satyrs, nymphs, vampires, mer-folk, etc., are capable of experiencing the primal self through the use of the shapeshifter's rituals. It is simply a matter of when, where, and how-to in order to become more than the ordinary self. Be safe in your practices and you shall reap the benefits of raising the kundalini and experience the heightened senses of the animal spirit within.

Testing Energy Work for Proof

An important aspect to consider for the coven of Otherkin is the testing of energy flows for talismans, created beings, crystal grids, etc. It seems that many people run entirely on "*faith*" in such items and yet they get to be rarely used or believed in by outsiders. So how do you KNOW when an item is charged and holding the energy that it is meant to contain? By performing simple tests among members as part of initiations or empowerment rites for crystals, etc., one can determine if the object is charged or not. One of the simplest tests that require only a little ingenuity is creating dowsing rods for the tests. Dowsing rods can be made of an old wire coat hanger and a small piece of cardboard from a paper towel roll. Cut the cardboard into small sections, only large enough that your hand can hold the cardboard without touching the wire. Then wrap the piece around the wire and tape it together to make a small tube. Bend the wire into an "L" shape with the longer end pointing away from you, and slip the cardboard onto the short end to make a handle. This way people can't say that you are manipulating the wire with your hands, as your palm will not touch the wire, only the cardboard. Do this for each dowsing rod that you make, and use them for the testing.

To use the dowsing rod for the test, simply hold the rods close to the item that is supposed to be charged, and watch the end of the rods. My own experimentation with this shows that when an item is charged, the rods will cross at the end, and if not will either remain still or twist away from each other. This can also denote a flow of energy on forest paths and roads. Of course, if you want, you can also buy an EMF meter for checking energy, but I donot know if they will pick up the subtle charge that a witch will place on an object. Haunted items may be the same but I haven't gotten to experiment with that yet.

Chapter Two
Following the Moon

The moon has always played a key role with those who identify with magical and spiritual practices. Ranging from the Moon Goddess of most witchcraft and Wiccan traditions, to the lunar magic of many native tribes, the moon holds many mysteries and powers that magicians and occultists have sought for millennia. To *"Follow the Moon,"* does not necessarily condone *"worship,"* but to spiritually align the self and magical workings with the darkness and lunar mysteries in order to attain the spiritual states we seek. Following the Moon is the way of the mage, the Otherkin sorcerer and the infernal shaman, no matter what their gender.

Our ancient and primal ancestors saw the moon and sun as the true forms of the gods they worshipped. The moon was recognized in many parts of the world as the sacred feminine and aligned with women's mysteries of birth, life, death and menstruation. In modern times, we have arrived in a scientific period, where we realize that these are other celestial bodies, like our Earth, in their natural alignment in our solar system and in the universe. With scientific thought these days, it's really no wonder how mankind has grown distant from the workings of the Moon and Sun. Yet there is always room for mystical and spiritual experiences under the influence of the Moon, as crime rates rise and mental hospitals have more problems during the time of the full moon. The powers of the moon can cause us to become easily excited or lethargic and depressed. We can feel the romance of candlelight under a full moon, or let out our inner beast. The moon will always have an influence upon us, no matter how scientific we think we are, or how superstitious we believe our pagan ancestors were. The moon is our guide through the darkness of night and our source of healing, empowerment and inspiration when in need upon our path. The moon acts as a beacon on the shore, to call us back to the wisdom of the dark and mystical realms of spiritual consciousness, where we can again attain the spiritual and magical powers our ancestors experienced. Whether you see the moon as the Goddess from Wiccan traditions or as Grandmother or Sister moon of native tribes, we can learn to align our spirits and our magical workings with the powers of the moon as well as the spirits and daemons that align with Her. Following the moon is to honor and connect with the rabbit or hare as a totem, which takes us down the rabbit hole, into other realms of being and with great fertility at our side.

For the coven of Otherkin, aligning with and following the moon will help to give greater structure to your practice, the coven, and will raise your inner awareness of the effects of the moon that happens to all of us. Working with rituals such as the classic *"Drawing Down the Moon,"* can be highly beneficial to us in more ways than we may realize. Aligning our energies and lunar magic throughout the year's cycle will increase our understanding of how energy works and can enable us to break through the fears and barriers that hold us back from a better life as Otherkin.

Moon Phases & Magical Rites
Dark & New Moons /Waxing and Waning

Working with the phases of the moon is nothing new in the world of magical practices. Achieving an understanding of the deeper aspects of each moon phase is something that often comes with age and years on the path. As we align ourselves with these varying energies of each month, we begin to create short-term patterns that allow us to achieve certain goals over time. Each pattern will only last through the twenty-eight day cycle of that lunar month. We are then given time during the waning moon to cleanse, purify, and clear away the negative energies, attain understanding of the cycle, and take the time to renew our selves before beginning in the next lunar month. Our understanding of magical and spiritual practices will be enhanced each time we pay attention to and follow the moon phases.

The phase of the dark moon is often overlooked unless being used for malevolent magic. The dark of the moon is the time before the new moon's crescent is visible, often thought to be a time of no moon. Usually there is a three-day period in which the moon is barely or not visible and can be used for a variety of different magical workings. This is a time of shadow energy and learning to use our shadows for beneficial work can be achieved more easily during the dark moon. The dark moon is the time just before birth, when creations are being made ready for emergence, into the light of the world. This is the transformation from one plane of existence to another. This lunar phase is also aligned with the death aspects or "*dark gods/goddesses*" of many different paths. The dark gods or spirits are those that destroy things first, in order to make room for a new creation. Their words speak of endings and they remain compassionate through putting a stop to suffering and offer spiritual liberation at the end of the cycle. Darkness allows us to be aware of negative aspects of whatever we are doing and to pay attention to the darkness in others and our selves as well. Many different totems, such as the owl, cougar, wolf and others, that teach us how to accept the cycles of life and death through making change, inhabit the darkness of night. Learning to use shadow energy can be beneficial for remaining unnoticed, creating forms for artificial creatures, or learning how to destroy in order to create anew. The dark moon is also a time of looking into the future and giving rise to the inner psychic sight. We can practice with divination devices during this time, as the dark moon becomes the darkened mirror or pool for scrying, and the outcomes of the runes are foretold by Skuld of the coming lunar cycle. The cycles of birth and death are inextricably tied to the darkest phase of the moon.

The new moon is the time of beginning and renewal in the lunar month. It grants us a time to start new projects and nurture them through the cycle into fruition at the full moon. If the dark moon is the crone, and symbolic of death, then the new moon is the maiden, fresh with life and fertility, and eager to grow forth. Looking into our projects, both spiritual and physical and where they lie at this time can give us insight into the ways things are being created at that particular time in our life. Whether we have set things in motion or are spiritually tricked into new beginnings, this is one of the best times for a new start in whatever our endeavors may be. Relationships, new jobs and career changes, moving into a new home, etc, can be influenced by the growing moon and enhanced if we consider the moon phases and time them appropriately to begin with the new moon.

Throughout the lunar months, the moon moves from dark to new moons, and waxes until the time of the full moon. The growing moon phase, from new to full, is the time for our many projects and spiritual practices to grow as well. This is the time to nurture our new creations and to see them through to fruition. If we follow the moon phases in our life, we will see many things grow to there fullest, before beginning the decline into change again. The questions or concerns, spells etc., vocalized or made aloud during the new moon, will be answered or completed by the full moon, before descending back into the darkness. The waning moon is the time of growing shadows and will let us adjust accordingly if we need this energy in our life. The darkening moon lets us rest in shadow before being thrust outward again into the light of new creation. It is easy to compare the lunar month, with the cycle of seasons in each year. The spring is the time of the new moon, the time of growth and fertility. The waxing moon is its movement towards the summer and the full moon is its height. The waning moon passes the summer and becomes the season of fall/ autumn and the dark moon is the darkness and cold of winter's grip.

Continuing the path we started during the new moon, we watch our ambitions, becoming reality, and our dreams, become our life. The full moon is the time of our greatest power and achievement. This is the middle point of the lunar month's cycle. This is easily translated as our time to shine and light the way for those around us. After the passing of the full moon, we again decline into the waning moon, which gives us time to cleanse and purify, preparing our selves for the returning of death and rebirth at the end of the moon's monthly cycle. As with all things, it will continue with or without our connection to the moon's monthly pull upon our psyche and soul.

As a last note in this section, with the technology available today, we have the ability to gain exact hours and times for different ruling planets, so as to align our magic and spells. This can be a wonderful aid to the serious practitioner of magic, without having to calculate for several hours to figure out when the moon's hour is in alignment with a certain day of the week. This can also aid us in opening to the energies of the other planets such as Jupiter, Venus, Saturn etc., as they move through stages of power throughout the day and night. Check the Internet for resources and programs that will be of benefit when working with lunar phases and planetary magic.

Working with Lunar Spirits & Daemons

The spirits of the moon are vast in number and can be called upon to affect a myriad of areas of life. From trickster spirits and faeries, to Mother Goddesses, to spirits of love, witchcraft, and death, all are under the dominion of the moon. Lunar spirits have been a part of pagan cultures for millennia and play an enormously important role in the magical community. Working with Lunar spirits is central to many traditions of witchcraft and paganism as well as other religions around the world. The Moon in all her many aspects, allow for a great number of attributes to be known and worked with in confidence by the practicing witch or magician. Lunar daemons tend to be less well known in the occult and magical community, while they do exist and are easily approachable by the adept practitioner. Amongst the many grimoires from ancient and modern times, I have found thirteen different daemons with some identification as lunar spirits ranging from an ancient triple goddess, to a succubus, and a king and many of his ministering spirits. In honesty, if we really look at some of the other daemon attributes amongst the grimoire traditions, any spirit that can aid in divination practices, or *"answers truthfully about matters of the past, present and future,"* should be considered to have a connection to the moon. While I have not had time yet to work with all of these spirits, I will list them and their attributes here for you to decide if and when you wish to work with them in lunar rites for the Otherkin practices.

Enepsigos – daemoness of the moon, said to have a triple form, connecting her to an ancient goddess, summoned to aid in drawing down the moon rites.

Harthan – daemon King of the Spirits of the Moon, element of water and the west quadrant, power to change people's thoughts and help with journeys. Also said to bestow strength and resolve, avenge wrongs, and provide darkness. I am currently under a daemon pact with Harthan, who appears to me in journeys as a man with a deer's head, full rack of antlers, and has a great sense of humor. I cannot divulge the circumstances of the pact at this time. On my first journey to Harthan, I received a personal sigil to contact him, or to connect with his energy through spells.

sigil of Harthan

Under King Harthan are several servants and ministers, with similar attributes. Of course, depending on which edition and from whom, as always true to the grimoire tradition. These spirits are —

Abuchaba – servant of Harthan can also call rains
Arnochap – same as above
Ayylalu – same as above, appeared to me in a journey with Harthan, as a Very black skinned African man that glowed with a bright white aura. He gave me a personal sigil for contact.

sigil of Ayylalu

Habnthala -- same
Hebethel -- same
Milalu – same
Milau – same
Asmoday (Asmodai, Asmodeus) – as "Asmodai" daemon connected to the moon, can make people

invisible, show the whereabouts of hidden treasure, can teach many arts

Lassal – daemon tied to the moon and its powers, summoned in a spell intended to take a person's will.

Onoskelis – daemoness tied to the moon, succubus daemon *"who seduces men to kill them."* Appeared to me in journey as a beautiful half-woman, half-spider daemon in a cavern, very friendly and can raise your kundalini by proximity, i.e., extremely sexual vampire spirit. She also gave me a beautiful symbol for contacting her that was more beautiful and artistic than expected.

sigil of Onoskelis

The flame in her sigil was blue but I would suggest visualizing the color rather than adding it to the image.

Onoskelis can teach vampirism and sexual allure to those that come to her honestly. Her totem is the spider.

Sariel – may have been as a *"Watcher"* from the *"Book of Enoch"* said to have taught knowledge of the phases of the moon to mankind after the fall of the angels, so may be called upon for the same purpose.

I know that there are many more daemons as well as pagan spirits that can be listed here, especially that are attributed to the moon. If we consider the western quadrant of the magic circle, as attributed to the moon, then any and all water spirits and spirits of death can be quickly added to this listing. But I didn't set out to write another dictionary, so we will keep this list short for our purposes. Understand that you can use any lunar spirits or deities, pagan gods, goddesses or daemons from the grimoires that you are comfortable calling upon for your spiritual and magical practice.

For those that can perform shamanic journey, you may wish to journey to those spirits that appeal to you or consult your guides to know which spirits to contact and which ones to avoid for your greatest benefit.

In working with the spirits of the moon, we need to keep in mind the changes that occur in each month, season, year, and moon phase. The Mother/Fertility Goddess aspect of the spring and summer moons are not the same as the dark, Crone or death aspects of the Blood Moon in October. Nor is the energy of the full moon the same now as it was ten or twelve years ago for older practitioners. The changes we go through in life will have an effect on how we relate to the moon in all of its phases. This can be a source of difficulty for long-term practitioners and needs to be relieved. For the purposes of this work, I will try to keep each monthly ritual from being too repetitive. This can be another difficulty in coven gatherings, as the rituals grow to be the same thing each month, the members get bored and slowly quit showing up. If we create living rituals that have a flow to them, it is less likely to feel like the same old thing over and over. For those new to the idea of living ritual, this can require some knowledge from the participants, but is well worth the effort. Living ritual is a way of writing ritual that only gives a basic structure to the rite, rather than every word for liturgies, invocations etc, being written down and memorized. It comes down to the ritual participants knowing what is to be done when, and trusting in each other to say the correct words at the proper time, without rehearsing and memorizing. This is a bit challenging at first but can be the difference between long-term covens and six months to finding new members.

The Blue Moon – Looking Ahead for Fun

Most of us have heard the phrase, *"once in a blue moon,"* but people outside of the pagan and magical communities, rarely understand the meaning behind it. The blue moon is the second full moon in one calendar month, which doesn't happen all the time, hence the old saying. It may be seen as the thirteenth moon that falls in different places each year, sometimes skipping a year, according to the calendar. The Blue Moon is intended as a time of revelry, enjoyment and doing something new or unique. In order to keep up with this ever-changing full moon, we need to keep a close watch on our calendar, to know when it will come around and give us a new opportunity.

Rituals of the Blue Moon may be aligned as according to the time of year that it falls, as a Blue Moon rite in summer, will differ from the Blue Moon rituals of winter. For Blue Moon rites, we may wish to look into what is going on in our lives at the time and plan accordingly for what we most need out of the Blue Moon's energy. This could be anything from a healing ritual that we have postponed or finding a new relationship/love interest in our life. We may wish to increase our financial gains through a new career or a change in position within our current employment. Again, these are just for ideas as to what can be done for our *"once in a Blue Moon"* rituals.

During the waxing time of the Blue Moon, we may wish to experience something new, rather than working it all into a ritual practice. Things that we have never done before can be experienced under the guidance of this moon. From taking a skiing trip in winter, to finally making our selves go skinny-dipping in spring or summer, the energy of the Blue Moon can be used as a protective measure while exploring parts of life and the world that we have neglected or just never been able to do.

For those that really want to work with the Blue Moon and take the plunge into something new, it may just be a matter of time before we get to work with the wild energy that the Blue Moon brings into our life and the world.

Chapter Three
January – The Wolf Moon

We start off the year of lunar rites with the full moon of January. This full moon is named *"the Wolf Moon,"* by some native tribes and rightfully so, as this is the time in which many parts of the country are covered in snow, making hunting among wolf packs difficult. This is often a time when wolves will tend to move closer to human habitation for food, whether to pick off livestock, family pets, or to dig through scraps and leftovers that are left out by people. On our modern calendar, the beginning of January is only about two weeks into the dead of winter, meaning that this is a time of inner work, contemplation and solace.

The beginning of winter at the solstice or Yule, at one time meant that life took on a totally different meaning. Our ancient forest dwelling ancestors knew that during the winter was time to hunt only when necessary, and livestock were killed to store the meat early for the winter. Vegetables and crops were traded or stored for food during the harshness of this time of year. The Wolf Moon is a time of inner work to contemplate what roots will be started in the months to come, within our life and within the world around us.

Rituals of the Wolf Moon for the Otherkin coven or solitary practitioner, may take on many different traits at this difficult time of year. Full moon rites may be about setting goals for the future, and beginning new creations i.e., putting down new roots. If the practitioner has not decided upon what goals to set down for the self and life in the new year, then divination practices may be used during this dark time of year to help in determining what is needed for the practitioner's life and spirit. Sticking to the old idea of *"what is started at the new moon will reach completion at the full moon,"* may be a good idea when in doubt about one's future or worried about making decisions on things to come.

The Wolf Moon is also a time of inner solitude and for those that are not a part of a coven or may be spending time alone to determine their life path, this is an excellent time for deep meditation practices to begin as well. Spending your quiet time fire gazing for illumination of the spirit is another good practice in the long cold nights of January.

For the Otherkin coven that gathers in the cold under this moon cycle, rites to honor the Wolf totem as a teacher and guide may be in order. Shapeshifting rites for the Otherkin wolves can be added or be the focal point of this full moon night. Vampires and succubi will also be able to gather under the Wolf Moon to revel in the darkness for a little longer before the return of the growing light in early February.

Otherkin Wolf Moon Ritual

This ritual is written for the coven that seeks to follow the moon throughout the year as Otherkin. This is in no way the only way to perform a full moon rite and each of the rites in this book are written as a guide for those that wish to create their own rituals for Otherkin covens. These rituals are based in tribal aspects of witchcraft and not meant to resemble the classic Wiccan full moon rite. I will also try to create the ritual around a coven that is not so based in hierarchy as suggested earlier in this book, but using the title of priest/ess is easier to write and understand.

This ritual can be adapted to be performed in doors for those that do not have an area large enough outside to gather, or when weather doesn't permit it. The area is prepared with a Wolf medicine shield hanging on a stake placed into the ground, or on a wall within the gathering room. The coven members create a circle of stones or mark the circle with flour poured upon the ground or floor. If the area is large enough, a fire may be made in the center of the area and or torches lit around the circle for light for the ritual participants. For indoor rituals use candles about the room for illumination. An incense/smudge bowl of cedar, pine or sage may be burned to cleanse the area and ritual participants. Mugwort, wormwood, and willow may be burned for the pure shapeshifters coven as empowerment incense. Vampire covens may wish to just burn wormwood.

The priest/ess, leader or trusted member of the coven may perform cleansings for all involved and the area using the smudge bowl and a feather fan to waft the smoke over them before continuing the ritual work. A rattle can be used to purify the area, also. The ritual area should be cleansed and set up with a small altar table or space on the ground for tools to be held.

> *Rattle, feather fan and smudge bowl*
> *Incense or smudge wand*
> *Drum(s) if available*
> *Wand or staff*
> *Ritual hammer or axe*
> *Medicine shield for wolf totem (if available)*
> *Stones or flour for marking the circle*
> *Candles if indoors, fire pit if outside*

For the shapeshifters coven of mixed Otherkin shifters and totemists, the rite will center around honoring the wolf spirit, as a guide and teacher and shapeshifting amongst the coven should be the height of full moon's energy. For this type of ritual, the priest/ess, leader, or trusted member of the coven begins to speak from the center or the northern most part of the area. Ritual participants should be quiet during the rite to allow the ritual leader or priest/ess to be heard.

> *Priest/ess --"Upon this night of the Wolf Moon, we gather to honor the spirit of the wolf, that dwells within all of us!"*

Carrying a rattle and shaking it rhythmically, the priest/ess or ritual leader begins to walk clockwise about the circle marked physically upon the ground or floor. They walk the circle three times chanting...

> *I cast thee sacred circle of power,*
> *Focused here, from this hour!*
> *Contain the power for this rite*
> *Enchant this circle of full moon night!*

Upon completing the third circle, the priest/ess places the rattle down upon the altar. He/she picks up the wand or staff and moves to the eastern most point. He or she raises the wand/ staff and speaks...

> *"Unto the East, I call to the powers of Air!*
> *To winds that stir the mind*
> *Let our mind's be clear and pure*
> *As we become the inner beast!"*

The priest/ess now moves to the south and holds the wand or staff up in the air. And speaks...

> *"Unto the South, I call to the powers of Fire*
> *To the courage and passion of our hearts*
> *Let our strength rise and our heart be pure*
> *As we become the inner beast!"*

The priest/ess lowers the wand or staff and moves to the western corner of the circle. He/she, holds the wand or staff up high again and speaks...

> *"Unto the West, I call to the powers of Water*
> *Let our emotions be still and intuition run high*
> *May our connection to the Moon be pure,*
> *As we become the inner beast!"*

The priest/ess moves to the North of the circle, and raises the wand or staff once more.

> *"Unto the North, we call to the powers of Earth*
> *May we find stability in the Earth*
> *Let our wisdom be strong*
> *As we become the inner beast this night!"*

The priest/ess or ritual leader places the wand/staff back upon or near the altar. If a ritual axe or hammer is used and/or available, it should be held up high in front of the priest/ess, and then held in front of the Wolf Medicine shield, as the priest/ess or ritual leader speaks...

> *"Spirit Wolf, we call upon thee, upon this night of the full moon, to honor the spirit teacher that guides us! Let the Wolf spirit come forth from within us and teach us of the ways of nature, of survival and wisdom. Upon this night we raise our voices to honor the Great Wolf!"*

Coven members begin to howl softly as if in the distance, but growing louder as the energy rises. At this point a drumbeat begins. This may be from one drum or many as you have available. But at the height of the ritual energy let the drum beat carry the *"wolves"* to a frenzy.

At this point any coven members that are going to join in the shapeshifting ritual should be within the circle and all others will remain on the outside of the circle. Ritual participants should remain within the circle for the duration of the shapeshifting rite, and only step out of the circle in special circumstances. This rite can be clothing optional for the shapeshifters as according to the area and weather. The circle is intended to contain the energy for the shift to occur. This is a precaution as well to ensure the safety of all involved and for outsiders that may be near the gathering area. The Leader of the rite holds the ritual hammer or axe aloft and speaks again…

"By the powers of the Wolf Moon, we rise in form and shadow, to take on the inner beast within! Let our power rise and may we walk as the Wolf in wisdom upon this sacred night!"

A chant slowly grows among the group, raising the energy for shapeshifting in the circle.

Eyes of the Wolf, be as mine!
Instinct and intuition combine!

Now the ritual participants begin to breath heavily, howling, and drumbeats cause the participants to begin to dance wildly about the circle. The priest/ess may join if they so desire, but ensuring that they keep to a reasonable level of consciousness to help anyone that may need it during the rite. If there are ritual attendees that are not joining the shift, they may chant to help in raising the energy within the ritual from outside of the circle. A dance of wolves can go on for a period of time, considering that no one allows them selves to go overboard in the shifting of consciousness. As the ritual participants wear down, the circle can slowly diminish in size as people move out of the circle to return to ordinary consciousness. After all have returned to normal consciousness, the priest/ess allows the shapeshifting to come to a close and then the priest/ess or ritual leader comes forth to close the circle.

> *"We thank thee, spirits of the Elements*
> *For your Energy and wisdom this night*
> *We thank thee, Spirit Wolf!*
> *For this Shapeshifter's rite*
> *We ask that you will be as our guide*
> *In the coming months!*
> *Be with us in Heart and Mind*
> *And Let us hear your call upon the wind*
> *In Wisdom and Blessing! Hail Thee and Thanks!!"*

All coven members – "Hail Thee Spirit Wolf!"

The coven members may now join in celebration after a tiring ritual. Food and drink may be brought out for a feast, but be sure to clean up and clear the area afterward.

Drawing Down the Wolf Moon

Another ritual that can be performed under the Wolf Moon is a rite of Drawing Down the Moon. As this lunar month is about inner work and contemplation, Drawing Down the Moon may be perfect for those that need the inner guidance or that seek to deepen their meditation skills, while attaining a connection to the Moon as a guide. The Wolf spirit may still be honored as a guide and teacher, being connected to the moon and being able to take the ritual participants deep into themselves to attain the spirit guidance that is needed.

I know that the classic rite of Drawing Down the Moon is from Wiccan/ witchcraft traditions and some people may not understand the combination of shamanism and witchcraft for such a ritual. The witchcraft aspect is in the ritual work, the circle casting, invocation of elementals at each corner, the invocation to the Moon Goddess and then begins the shamanic practice. Within the sacred circle, the shaman and/or the ritual participants are seated or laying and using the rhythm of the drum and rattle to journey into the Otherworld to speak to the Moon Goddess, or other beings to attain the knowledge that is sought within the ritual. This gives the ritual a powerful boost, rather than only being worked in the physical realm. The spiritual aspect is embraced and the boundary between worlds is crossed through shamanic journey, until the end of the rite. Then the elementals and deities are thanked for guarding the circle and the circle is closed in the usual formal way.

This ritual is written from a shamanic perspective and utilizes the ability to journey with a drum and/or rattle. This is a ritual for indoors, as it is less active in its physical approach and more intent on attaining shamanic consciousness to travel between worlds for knowledge and guidance in what is going on in the participant's life. If one amongst the group is a practicing shaman, this will make things less complicated and the shaman can be as a guide for the other ritual participants. As a practicing shaman myself, I feel that it is easier to drum for myself, as it gives an amount of control to the ritual consciousness. This allows me to decide when to speed up or slow down the rhythm to induce further trance and travel.

For the purposes of altering this ritual, I will leave out the invocations of the elements at each corner, and you can decide whether to invoke the elements for your circle or not. Shamanic journey doesn't require extensive invocations for the journey to work, but it can add extra energy to the circle, which may give the participants the extra energy needed. This rite can also be created as a healing rite, or ritual initiation during this time of year, by altering the journey itself. For healing or initiation rites, the shamanic practitioner in the group journeys alone to retrieve the energy of a lunar spirit to connect the recipient more energetically to lunar powers for the healing or initiation and brings it back and blows it into the recipient's crown chakra. The shamanic practitioner then completes the journey by bringing them selves back to ordinary consciousness and brings the drum to rest. Then the ritual circle will be closed as usual.

For this ritual, only a few items are really needed, but other tools may be applied as the coven or group see fit.

>*Drum & rattle*
>*Smudge wand of cedar or sage, or incense*
>*Blankets to lie on and/or for warmth*
>*1 White candle*
>*Wolf Medicine shield (if available)*
>*Journals or notebooks (for notes afterward)*

The candle may be placed in the center of the circle area, and participants lay or sit around the circle. The shaman leading the rite will need enough space to move behind and /or around the individuals within the circle and move back to his/her seat. If desired the group may be cleansed in the smudge prior to the ritual beginning. Let the medicine shield be hung on a wall or propped up on the altar area to be seen by all in attendance.

To begin the shaman stands and speaks the intent, before moving into the circle casting.

>*"Upon this night, we gather to call upon the Moon Goddess, and we ask Her for her blessing upon this circle and in our lives. On this Sacred Night of the Full Moon, we gather to honor the Great Wolf Spirit, our teacher and guide through our life and spirit realms! May we be cleansed and empowered within this circle, as we take the Spirit*

Journey, to seek the answers we need within our life.
Hail thee, Mother Moon! Hail thee Spirit Wolf! Be
with us in this Circle Cast, Grant us your wisdom!"

The coven may respond with …
"Hail thee Mother Moon! Hail thee, Spirit Wolf!"

The shaman ignites the smudge and begins to walk the circle, being sure to go outside of all participants in the rite. He/she, makes the circle with the smudge wand, giving a blessing within the circle, then picks up the rattle and walks the circle again, to remove any negative energy and bless the circle. He/she begins a shamanic chant to empower the circle, casting the energy as they walk. After the circle is cast, the shaman or another priest/ess, may light the candle in the center of the group. The shaman picks up the drum, and begins a slow heartbeat rhythm. The shaman speaks again…

"Mother Moon, We call thee, into this circle
That we may share in your wisdom!"
"I invoke the Mother Moon!
I invoke thee Spirit Wolf!"

Low howls may be heard through the group as the drum begins to speed up in tempo. This signals the beginning of the journey phase of the ritual. The shaman may control the rhythm as needed to induce the trance and take everyone in attendance into the journey. The shaman may chant during part of the journey or simply let the drum carry the trance. Journeys can take anywhere from thirty minutes to an hour if need be, but after that it gets difficult to maintain the trance and drumming together. Towards the end of the journey, the shaman signals the call back with a series of rapid drum beats followed by a short silence. Then the drumming will begin again to allow for closure of the rite and bringing everyone back to normal consciousness. When the shaman sees that everyone is back into normal consciousness, the drumming may slow to a stop and let everyone write down there journey experience before closing the rite.

The shaman stands, before the candle in the center of the gathering and raises the candle into the air.

> *"We thank thee Blessed Moon, for your guidance through the Otherworld. May your wisdom be shared among us, and bring us knowledge upon our path in this life. Blessed Wolf Spirit, we thank thee for guiding us through the Otherworld, may you guide and bless us in our lives and grant us wisdom upon our path. Hail Thee! Hail Thee!!"*

The candle is extinguished and the rite is ended. Those in attendance may speak about what they saw or experienced in the Otherworld to gain an understanding from the shaman's perspective, about interpreting the many realms outside of this world.

Chapter Four
February – Storm Moon & Imbolc

The month of February brings with it the renewal of the power of the sun, of cleansing and purification, as well as an opening of the heart to those we love. With the celebration of Imbolc/Candlemass/Groundhog Day on or about February 2, the power of the rising sun is revealed and honored. Also in this month, is the holiday of Saint Valentine's Day on the 14th which, is our modern celebration of the season and spirits of love. It may seem a bit ironic that the full moon of this month is called "Storm Moon," yet it is a time of change and preparation for the spring and sometimes of relieving winter's unrelenting grip upon the land.

In pagan times, the celebration of Imbolc was a fire festival to honor the return of the sun and the lengthening of the hours of daylight. We must keep in mind that all pagan celebrations were centered around the harvest cycles of the Earth itself. If the winter's ferocity continued longer into February, the time of planting was postponed and could for the early people's represent a difficult year. The name of the month, "February," is a reference to a type of divination practiced by tribal people, which required reading the entrails of cattle or livestock. This shows that there may have been concerns about weather changes at this time of year and divination was practiced to look into the future for the tribe. This tradition of practicing divination by watching animals carries on to modern times in the belief and practice of Groundhog Day. There were also many fiery and solar gods and goddesses worshipped at this time of year, in the hopes that spring would come soon to the land, to allow for planting and new growth to begin.

The Storm Moon is a time of cleansing and purification rites, for the self and home. The ideas of *"out with the old and in with the new,"* may come from this time of year. The Storm Moon brings about a time of preparation for spring as the winter subsides and new growth begins. Storms represent periods of fertility brought about by rains and may also represent destruction to clear the way for new growth. The roots that we put down in January's Wolf Moon, are still, or should be, growing and this is time to look for the emergence into the light, of whatever we have started to create in our life from the previous season. For the Otherkin that is a practicing totemist, a rite of honoring the Great Bear Spirit may be in order on Imbolc or the Storm Moon, as this symbolizes a time of coming out of hibernation in nature and regaining strength for the coming year.

For the coven of Otherkin, the rite of Imbolc may be performed in the morning and if you can, gather to watch the rising sun upon this day. Many modern witch's rites are centered around gathering at night but I believe our ancestors once understood the need for a balance of night and day, depending upon the time of year and reason for the gathering. For the covens that wish to gather by night, a bonfire can built as according to traditional beliefs and practices. Otherkin covens may wish to gather to perform rites of purification and cleansing in homes and upon each other at this time of year. In keeping with the magical reasons for gathering, the Otherkin coven may also want to perform initiations or power animal retrievals at this time of year, as a way of honoring the renewal of light, i.e., passing on wisdom and knowledge.

The month of February brings with it multiple opportunities for rituals of cleansing, growth, renewal and love for the practitioner of the Otherkin path or member of an Otherkin coven. These rites may be performed as they are, or in unison together, depending on how the Storm Moon falls between or on Imbolc and Valentine's Day in coming years.

Otherkin Imbolc Ritual

In honoring the return of the sun and the lengthening of daylight, plan to gather just before dawn. If you have a fairly large group, you may wish to try to time the ritual to completing the cleansing and purification before sunrise. You may wish to make it a place where the coven can watch the sunrise together as the ritual begins.

Needed: Sage or cedar Smudge wand or loose herbs
    Stoneware bowl or shell
    Large piece of Citrine/Sunstone (if possible)
    Feather fan
    Drum (s) and beater
    Rattle

Large pillar candle (white or yellow)
Bear totem image or medicine shield

Before the rite begins, the ritual items should be in the center of the area for the circle. Place the pillar candle in the center with the Citrine/Sunstone close by. If you have a stand for the Medicine shield, it should be standing inside the circle as well. Other items will be placed near by within the circle for ease of use. See the image on the following page for a representation of the set up of the circle gathering for Imbolc. This is a basic structure for a shamanic ritual and other items may be added or changed as needed.

All coven members will join in the center of the circle to be cleansed prior to completing the ritual working. To begin the rite, the priest/ess, shaman or trusted member of the coven, picks up the smudge wand and faces the East to the early glow of the sunrise, and ignites the smudge. As he/she blows into the smudge wand and the smoke begins to fill the air, the priest/ess cleanses themselves then moves to the next member. If the coven has both a priest and priestess, then they may wish to perform the cleansing for each other, before moving to the first member of the coven. For the cleansing, begin at the feet and blow the smudge towards them, then move up the legs, lower abdomen, across the chest, down the arms, and up to the shoulders and finally the head. If you have time, or have a small group, the blessing from the smudge may be the Nine-Fold Blessing of each foot, loins, each breast, each hand, lips and third eye.

After the cleansing is complete for all members, the priest/ess or shaman begins to cast the circle. If this is timed before daybreak is perfect. All members need to be within the circle area as the shaman performs the circle casting. Rattling around the area as he/she walks the shaman or priest/ess chants to raise and send the energy for the circle.

> *"I cast thee sacred circle of power*
> *Focused here from this hour!"*

After walking the circle three times while rattling and chanting, the shaman or priest/ess moves to the center of the circle and raises the candle to the now rising sun and speaks as a slow rhythmic drum beat begins...

> *"We gather this morning to honor the return of*
> *the Sun and the Renewal of the Light. Let the Sun*
> *bring us many blessings, as we grow throughout*
> *this year. By the light of the Candle, we bring the*

light of the sun into our lives and spirits. Hail Thee, Lord of the Sun!"

The coven members repeat, *"Hail thee Lord of the Sun!"* The priest/ess or shaman lights the candle and places it back into the holder in the center of the gathering. Now the priest/ess raises the Citrine/Sunstone and speaks...

"By the power of the sacred stone, let the Sun shine upon our lives, and release us from winter's grip. May we awaken from our hibernation, to bring our spirits and powers from the darkness and let them be revealed in the sun's warmth and light! Hail thee to the Great Bear Spirit! As he awakens from his slumber, and comes forth from his cave, may we attain the powers to be as the Great Bear and step forth into the light of a new day in this beautiful dawn! Hail thee Great Bear!!

The coven calls, "Hail thee Great Bear!"

The priest/ess holds the stone up to the Medicine shield and lowers his/her head in honor. Coven members lower their heads to honor the Bear Spirit, as a totem and spiritual teacher. The drum beat in the background now gets louder as the stone is placed in the center of the gathering and the coven members may begin to dance in the light of the morning sun. After a time of dancing, the group may wish to perform initiations or power animal retrievals for new members of the coven. Journeys or healing rites can be performed for those who need or desire it, or the shaman or priest/ess may speak about the many things the Bear teaches us as a totem. When all is finished the priest/ess or shaman may close the circle as usual.

I know that many more things can be done for the Imbolc rite, invocations of the elements, God and Goddess candles and invocations, as well as honoring gods and goddesses of hearth and fire. But the point for these rites is to honor the cycles of the earth, and use that time for magic, healing and learning. The time of Imbolc is about preparations for the spring and what roots have been planted in the fall and winter months before.

Otherkin Storm Moon Ritual

Rituals of the Storm Moon should be focused on clearing, cleansing and purification, as well as removing blockages that keep our roots from growing. In this time of renewal, we can use the energy of the Storm Moon and the rising power of the Sun to clear the way for our dreams to come into fruition and begin bringing them into the physical world. If our roots are weak or are not being nurtured, or are blocked in some way, we can plan to magically change this situation during the Storm Moon ritual. If you are unsure about the state of your "roots" you may wish to perform some divinations to see what information you receive and decide what action to take. Read your favorite set of tarot cards, a set of bones, runes, scrying or any other divination to attain the information that you seek.

When you know what is happening with the roots of your present situation, you can plan accordingly for the full moon. You may need to make a representation of your problem area to remove it magically during the ritual. This may be ritually cast away into the air or water, buried in the earth or burned in a ceremonial fire to remove the problem. Healing rituals may also be planned for the coven gathering to aid in each members growth within the coven and within their life. Healing rites should be for the nurturing aspect, while removing blockages are for allowing roots to grow. Some things and people may be in need of both nurturing and removing blockages, as from within the self. Fears and wrong ideas can be just as much a block in our own life path as a boulder or a person who stands in our way. Be sure to search deep within when finding out the state of the roots in your life and be honest with your self.

To begin this ritual, you may wish to perform a cleansing again with the smudge wand upon each member of the coven prior to the working. After all members have been properly cleansed, the priest/ess or shaman of the group gathers the needed items and begins the circle casting. Each member may wish to have a personal item available as representation of their blockages or needs for nurturing. This is written for using a fire to burn away what blocks our path, but this may be changed as according to your groups needs. Gathering by a natural water source such as a lake, river or the ocean, would allow members to release the items into the water, so long as the items are natural and will break down without polluting the water source. Make figures of natural clay or mud and sticks for this. Other options are available with a little imagination.

Needed: Smudge wand or loose herbs and bowl
    Personal Items for removing blocks
    Fire pit or campfire
    Drum(s) and beater
    Blankets for seating and warmth
    Rattle
    Coven Medicine shield (if available)

When setting up the ritual area, make the fire pit or campfire the center of the rite. The priest/ess or shaman begins to cast the circle, walking the area three times with the rattle, chanting and casting energy.

> *"I cast thee sacred circle of power*
> *Focused here from this hour*
> *Contain the power for this rite*
> *Enchant this circle on full moon night!"*

After the circle is cast, the priest/ess or shaman moves to stand by the fire and faces the group. A slow drumbeat begins in the background as he/she holds their hands up to the rising moon and begins to speak...

> *"Upon this night we call upon the power of the*
> *Storm Moon. Mother Moon, grant us your blessing*

*and guidance in removing what blocks our path,
as individuals and as a whole within this coven.
Let us grow forth and become empowered in our
life with wisdom and inner strength. We focus this
night upon our roots, to grow and be nurtured
that we may grow as well. Grant us your Blessing
Mother Moon!"*

The drum begins to beat faster as each member of
the coven moves towards the fire one at a time. As they
reach the fire, they say a short prayer or incantation as
they throw in the representation of what blocks their path
then they move out of the way so the next in line can do
the same. The priest/ess or shaman will be the last one
in the line to remove their blockages. As the priest/ess
or shaman casts their item to be removed into the fire,
they cast extra power to aid the incantations of all other
members of the coven.

> *"By the powers of Fire
> All burns away
> I remove what blocks
> Our paths this day!
> Let us grow
> By root and seed
> To be strong upon
> The paths we lead!"*

After the priest/ess or shaman completes the first
chant, the rest of the group may join in to raise more

power together. Continue the chanting for a time then, the shaman or priest/ess may begin performing healing rites for individuals amongst the coven members. When the healing rites are complete, the coven members may dance for a while to the drumming to raise their own energies and integrate the powers from the ritual. When the dancing has slowed, the priest/ess or shaman may close the circle after a final blessing.

> *"Mother Moon! We thank thee for your guidance upon this night! May we be blessed in the light of a new dawn within our lives, and remove what blocks our paths. Hail thee Mother Moon! And thank you for honoring us upon our path of spiritual growth! Hail thee Storm Moon!"*

The coven calls, *"Hail Thee Storm Moon!"*

The priest/ess or shaman closes the circle and the ritual is done.

Calling Upon Spirits and Daemons of Love

The day of February 14th has become the American celebration of love, romance, and relationships. There is much debate as to the origins of this holiday, some claiming it to be from early Christianity and a priest that allowed men and women to be married against the Emperors rule. Others say that it is an attempt from Christianity at overthrowing or displacing the Greco-Roman pagan celebration of Lupercalia, on February

15th. At any rate, Valentine's Day is celebrated as a day of love and romance and this energy can be utilized for the Otherkin coven to attain their own needs.

There are many spirits and daemons that Otherkin practitioners can call upon that correspond to issues of love, lust and romance amongst the many pagan traditions and pantheons from other religions. The following list is of spirits that come from the grimoire traditions and while typically named as *"daemons"* are helpful to those that contact them with an open heart and sincerity. Not all of these spirits are directly related to matters of love, but may be called upon for a magical boost in terms that go with love, lust and desire.

Anteros – Greek spirit of love, name means *"love returned"*

Asafoetida – daemoness of feminine attributes

Ashtaroth – priestess/daemoness of friendship and divination

Asmodeus – daemon of lust

Astarte – pagan goddess mentioned in the grimoires, daemoness of love and soulmates

Gremory – while a not spirit of love exactly, a daemon of the water element that offers gain in all aspects of life including love and wealth

Rashoon – daemoness of seduction

Rosier – daemon of love, self-love and long-term relationships

Saleos/Sallos – daemon of earth element and love

Taroon – daemoness of desire

Unsere – daemoness of fertility and sorcery, Her sacred month is February

As you can see from this list, there are a number of spirits that one can work with in these matters and may be used throughout the month or year as the practitioner needs or desires. Be truthful about what you really seek and they may bless you in ways you never imagined.

Ritual for Valentine's Day

While a ritual for Valentine's Day is definitely not customary, it is not entirely unheard of either. This is a national day for love and romance, and indeed using the energy in the air can aid those who seek to find their true mate in life. This ritual can be created for finding a new love in your life or making your feelings known to your special someone. This may also be a day used by lovers who share the same beliefs to conjure up more energy sexually. For the Otherkin coven gathering, this is a rite of opening the heart chakra and removing what blocks us from living with an open heart in daily life. This is not about being sentimental or emotional, but about attaining a clear mind and an open heart, to see the world from a different set of eyes, as well as opening the heart to see the beings of the Otherworld, the fairies and elves, as they cross into ours.

The coven may wish to gather before sunrise in the early morning or in the afternoon before sunset to set up the area. Meditations will need to be performed prior to the rite, to have a greater success rate for clearing the mind and opening the heart chakra. This rite is intended to aid each member of the coven in opening the heart and seeing through the true eyes, into the Otherworld. Obviously, we won't all *"attain the sight,"* but we may be able to encourage the spirits of nature to grant their blessing upon our coven and upon our lives. Remember that if your coven uses a place in nature for this ritual, to try to use the same place each year, to charge the area for greater results in coming years. The energy added by rituals will give the area a new aura and energy and make contact with fairy beings more likely to happen.

> Needed: 7 quartz crystals (medium to large size)
> 1 large piece of rose quartz
> 4 green candles
> 4 pink candles
> Drum(s) and beater
> Fairy flowers or herbs such as roses, cardamom seeds, rosemary, thyme, carnations, orchids, etc; brought by coven members
> Flutes (if available)
> Wand or staff
> Flour or stones to mark the circle

Mark a fairly large circle carefully with flour or stones and create a seven-pointed star grid with the seven quartz crystals. Alternate in placing the green and pink candles within the grid and save one pink candle for the center, placed with the large piece of rose quartz. If the weather is warm enough, this rite may be performed nude or mostly nude, depending on your area and comfort level. After the area is set up, have all members of the coven stand around the outside of the circle being careful not to cross into it and then you may begin.

The priest/ess or shaman picks up the wand or staff to activate the crystal grid. See below for activation.

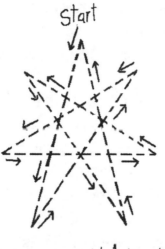

Septagram Grid Activation

Making a motion with the wand or staff in hand, the priest/ess or shaman of the coven, carefully traces the septagram sigil three times to activate its energy. At this point, the candles are lit from outside of the circle moving clockwise from the top point and lighting each one around the grid, then reaching into the center to light this candle last. When the grid is activated and all the candles are lit, the priest/ess moves to the top point of the grid and faces the coven members, which now encircle the area.

> *"Upon this day, we open our hearts to see in the in-between. May we be blessed with a clear mind and open hearts for all the creatures of the Earth.*
>
> *Spirits of this forest place*
> *You who tend this sacred space*
> *Join us in our revels true*
> *We come to open our hearts to you!"*

If a member of the coven plays a flute or pan pipes, they may begin to play a soft melody, letting it fill the forest area and bring a sense of peace and calm to all the members of the coven. Each member of the gathering that brought flowers and herbs should now move close to the circle and make an offering to the fairy spirits of the forest and place. They may ask for inner sight to see into the fairy realm or for something else that they need, but each person should be very sincere and as open hearted as they can manage to be. After all the offerings are placed within the circle, the flute grows quiet and the drum begins a slow steady beat. The coven members allow for a moment of silence, listening to the drum beat, and slowly the flute comes back into the music of the forest, and the coven members begin a dance to celebrate in the open heart of the moment. Allow the dance to go on for a time, then as members slow their dancing, other members of the coven may begin to take turns reciting poetry, or singing and dancing in the forest. Allow this rite to be about openhearted freedom and joy within the coven. This is one of the greatest ways of opening the heart and being free without fears or worries holding us back. The fairy spirits are there in the forest with you, if you can just open your heart enough to see them. Allow the candles to burn out, and be sure to leave the offerings in the circle after the crystal grid is deactivated and the crystals are removed. Be thankful to the spirits of this place where you sing and dance and they will grant you many blessings.

So where is the ritual structure and invocations to the elements and God and Goddess etc, etc, etc,? It is truly not needed on a day of love and devotion to life and opening the heart. The heart opens when we free ourselves from the trappings of daily life and even from the trappings of spiritual traditions. Spiritual power is within us, not necessarily in traditional means of *"worship."* Allow the rite to flow as love from your heart and you may attain a greater sight than you realize.

Chapter Five
March – Chaste Moon & Spring Equinox

The full moon of March is called the *"Chaste Moon"* and this is the time to prepare the earth for planting and our selves for new growth. This is the moon of the Maiden aspect and she points the way to beginning our outward growth into the sunlight, for plants as well as the projects that we have recently started. This is a time of preparation and nurturing for the new growth and abundance that is possible for the future. During the Wolf Moon of January, we set the roots and planned for what we would grow forth in the year to come. The Storm Moon of February gave us time to allow those roots to grow strong, to ensure their survival. Now with the coming of the Spring Equinox, we begin our outward growth and nurture whatever we have set in motion.

It is easy for the modern mind to get confused about what this really means. When we think of planting and preparation, we tend to think of the grandmother in our neighborhood, out digging in her garden, planting flowers to make her yard and home more beautiful. We will also think of the farmers out plowing fields to break the ground for their crops. Both of these types of planting are familiar and will be used in this model, but are not always what we need. This is the planting for the short-term goals, for beauty and food throughout the year. If we are truly to grow forth in our life in the year(s) to come, we must think about the perennial plants that remain through the cold months and survive the frost, like many herbs and trees. These are the plants that will teach us how to become perennial in our own growth and help us to create a foundation for continuous growth or "*fertilize the ground*" that our roots grow from.

Applying the knowledge of the cycles of the Earth to our own growth and change in life gives us a great model to represent how life and our new creations grow from the ground up. It is easy to understand that we must go within our self and have a plan to build upon, as represented by the *"roots"* we started in January. It is also easy to understand how giving ourself time to really formulate these plans relates to allowing the "*roots to grow stronger*," in the month of February. Now that the Spring Equinox is coming, this part of growth can be confusing for a society that has lost its connection to the agricultural and harvest based calendar of our pagan ancestors.

The Chaste Moon is the time for building upon what we have already started and to encourage and ensure its growth and fertility. Whether in starting a business and beginning to advertise it, or taking classes and preparing our selves for the tests to come, the Chaste Moon teaches us how to prepare for what will be in our future. This is classically considered a time of the fairy folk, when the nature spirits are the most easily seen and they may also be representative of where we are in our growth. The Maiden aspect that the Chaste Moon represents is the young woman in or about her teen years that has recently begun her menstrual cycle and is getting interested in things of the adult world. This is the time of becoming curious about the opposite sex (and sometimes even the same sex) and can be a time of difficulty both emotionally and physically, if not well prepared. I know that the average young woman in this day and age may only get some of the information that they need to get through this difficult time, and this also encourages us to plan better when working with this model in our lives. The youth that hasn't been prepared for the changes to come will have greater difficulty in growing forth in later years. So it is with our own growth and creations in life.

The Chaste Moon also represents the future aspects in divination. In the Norse runic tradition, Skuld is the Norn that foretells the future and she is considered the youngest of the three sisters. This is a great way to understand that the old do not determine the future, as there's have already been set in motion. It is in the youth that possibilities exist. So the Chaste moon is a time of the many possibilities, or fairies, for growth and change in the futures to come. This also creates a link between the practice of divination and the rituals for the Chaste Moon and Spring Equinox.

Daemons & Spirits of the Spring Equinox

There are many well-known deities in pagan traditions that correspond to the Spring Equinox and season. The following is a list of daemon spirits from the grimoire traditions and Daemonolatry community that are less known but will aid in the rites of divination and Spring. Other spirits such as those that help to bring rain for the season may be invoked and are listed earlier in the lunar spirits section of this book.

Ashtaroth – daemoness/priestess of friendship and divination

Azlyn – daemoness of divination

Beelzebuth – daemon of money, prosperity, luck

Belphegore – daemon of mastery, gain, armor, money

Delepitorae – daemoness of magick and sorcery, divination, spring is her season

Gremory – water daemon of gain in all aspects of life

Lucifer – literally, *"bringer of light,"* air elemental daemon of enlightenment and initiations, spring is his time

Verrier – daemoness of herbal knowledge and healing, can be called upon in late spring

Of course there are many more spirits that can be listed for the spring season and full moons, but I'll leave that research up to you. You may wish to work with the fairy spirits that have no real written information or invocations, or contact the spirits of your area in nature through shamanic journey practices, offerings and rituals.

Chaste Moon Ritual

For the Otherkin coven's Chaste Moon rite, you may wish to begin by performing divinations for each member, reading runes, tarot cards, bones, etc, prior to the ritual. This practice gives each member something to contemplate and understand about where he or she is in their life and perhaps where their life is going. Rituals and spells of abundance for the coming year can be performed with this ritual or you may opt for a spell to call spirits to bring rains for the earth's abundance and growth. For the Otherkin coven, this is a time of honoring the elves, fairies, satyrs, nymphs, etc, and this may be incorporated also. Either way, there are again many different possibilities for the full moon of Spring.

The following ritual is very non-traditional for full moon rites and is more directed toward honoring the spirits of nature and the earth her self. This includes a journey to the middle world to retrieve plant spirit totems for the coven to learn from. This rite may alternate with the Rite of the Spring Equinox if you wish.

    Need: Live plants (potted plants or herbs are fine)
        Drum(s) & beaters
        Rattle
        Blankets to lie on
        Smudge wand & bowl or shell
        Flour or stones to mark the circle
        Medicine shield (if available)
        1 green candle
            (or torches if you are outside)
        Offerings for nature spirits
            (honey, milk, herbs, etc)

Begin by physically marking the circle with stones or flour and have room for all ritual participants to lie on the blankets within the circle. The center of the circle should hold the green candle and live potted plants or you can make the circle around a tree. You may bring extra water if you are using a tree and water the tree after the ritual is complete. The priest/ess or shaman performs a cleansing on each participant beginning with their self, then all enter the circle as the priest/ess or shaman begins to cast the circle with the rattle and smudge. Walking the circle three times clockwise cleansing the space and casting energy by chanting or rattling the shaman or priest/ess makes a blessing over the area before completing it. After the circle is cast, with all participants seated within the circle, the shaman or priest/ess lights the candle in or near the center of the circle and makes the offering of the smudge to the four directions and above and below.

Facing the East, he/she holds the burning smudge up in the air and calls...

"I offer the sacred smudge to the East. Let us honor the growing light that illuminates our path, and warms us as we grow upon the Earth. Hail thee!"

He or she now turns and faces the South, and calls...

"I offer the sacred smudge to the South. Spirits of courage and light, be with us upon our path and guide us to clear seeing within the light. Hail thee!"

The priest/ess now turns to the West and raises the smudge…

> *"I offer the sacred smudge to the West. Spirits of intuition grant us the power to see within a clear mind and feel with our hearts! Hail thee!"*

The priest/ess or shaman now faces the North and raises the smudge again…

> *"I offer the sacred smudge to the North. Spirits of fertility and abundance, guide us to create the abundance we seek upon our path as we honor Mother Earth! Hail thee!"*

Looking up to the sky above, the priest/ess calls again…

> *"I offer the sacred smudge to the sky spirits. Mother Moon, I call to the Spirits of expansion and possibilities who look down upon us from above, guide our path and help us to see the great Earth in abundance and to understand our path in life. Hail thee!"*

The shaman or priest/ess now kneels to the earth with the smudge in hand and speaks…

> *"I offer the sacred smudge to Mother Earth. Spirits of Earth, grant us your blessing upon this night of the Chaste Moon, as we learn to walk in new ways to create a better world for the future.*

*Grant us your understanding in our minds and
hearts as we journey to the middle world tonight!"*

The shaman or priest/ess rests the smudge back into
the bowl or shell and lifts the drum and beater. All ritual
participants now lie within the circle as the shaman
begins a steady beat on the drum. He or she now sits and
speaks once more...

*"I journey this night of the Chaste Moon to the
middle world, to retrieve the plant spirit totems
for those who would seek it. Spirits of the middle
realm guide me and aid me in my journey!"*

The drumbeat now grows faster as the shaman or
priest/ess begins a journey to retrieve plant spirit totems
for those in the coven that have not yet received them or
that wish too. This part of the rite will take a lot of time
and energy if there are very many participants that are
undergoing the journeywork. Participants may journey
some with the shaman or priest/ess drumbeat but need
to be ready to receive the spirit when the shaman comes
to them.

After a time of the priest/ess or shaman journeying
for the coven, the members offerings may be made to the
nature spirits in the area and or water the tree(s) with the
water brought to the rite. When the shaman or priest/
ess is ready they may close the circle as usual. If you
used flour for the circle, you may leave it for food for the
ground and small animals and birds.

Plant spirit totems aren't as well documented as animal totemism today so it may take some time and patience to learn for members of the coven. This practice can help us to connect with nature and cycles of growth through the world of plants and trees. Look into the plants properties and magical correspondences for information about what each plant spirit can help us with. They may come to us to help in learning specific abilities or at times when we need to recognize healing potential, etc. You may wish to do further research and/or practice divination for your answers to help each individual to connect with their plant spirit totems. Be sure that you don't overlook agricultural and scientific information such as the plants survival tendencies during drought or high water conditions, needs for light and shade etc., as this may hold the key that you need to understand the plant spirits in your life.

Spring Equinox Ritual

The rite for the Spring Equinox should be performed during the morning hours if possible. In this way we honor the rising sun as well as the fertility and growth of the earth and nature around us. This practice also helps to honor the balance of nature in cycles of light and dark for the coven members. In this way we are neither, dark nor light, but we understand the place and need of both within the cycle of life and our self. For the Otherkin coven, this should be a time of reawakening as spirits of nature and being able to revel in life, love and the joys of spring.

If possible, hold the ritual outside in a field, in the forest or near a lake or river. For those who are daring, the rite may be performed nude or scantily clad, weather permitting, of course.

> Need: Light Green candles
>   (one for each member of the coven)
>   7 quartz crystals
>   Flour or stones for the circle
>   Offerings -- (Flowers, herbs or stones for spirits of place)
>   Crystal-tipped Wand
>   Drum(s) & beaters
>   Cedar smudge wand & bowl
>   Lighter or matches

Mark the circle with flour or stones and create the septagram crystal grid with the seven quartz crystals within it. The priest/ess or shaman casts the circle with the cedar smudge wand and then activates the crystal grid with the crystal-tipped wand. (See page 95 for activation) The ritual participants should be seated around the outside of the circle holding their candles and leaving space between the bottom two points of the septagram crystal grid. The priest/ess or shaman stands at the top point of the grid and speaks...

> *"We gather here this day to celebrate the sun and return of the Spring. For us, this is a time of our own spiritual renewal as Otherkin spirits amongst*

the Earth and humanity. By the re-growth of the Earth, we renew our kinship with our Otherkin spirits and the world of nature around us. To all those who would rise again as Otherkin, may they step through the circle of magick and be reborn."

The priest/ess or shaman enters into the center of the circle, walking in from between the bottom two points. This will be as the doorway for the circle for all members to pass through. If there is an active priest and priestess for the coven, they may step through the circle in turn and light each other's candles and speak as according to their way as Otherkin. Other members of the coven will have their candle lit by the priest/ess standing outside the circle at the top point of the grid. As the priest/ess or shaman enters, the drumbeat begins and should continue throughout the ritual until the offerings are made. You may need to have a member of the coven that can drum for the shaman and or priest/ess if available. This is a rite of renewing our own magical ties as Otherkin and reminding ourselves of what we are, while standing nude in the morning sun of the Spring Equinox.

Priest stands outside the circle holding the crystal-tipped wand with the priestess standing within the center of the magick circle. She holds her candle in her left hand and speaks …

"I enter the circle of life and magick, to renew myself as a spiritual Elf of the Otherkin! I walk the

*path of the elves within this life in spirit and honor
those spirits that guide me. Let me remain again
in this year as the Elf that resides within my soul
and continue upon my path. Hail Thee !!"*

The priest now lights her candle with a lighter or match
and grants her blessing by gently placing the crystal tip
of the wand upon her forehead. She then steps forward
through the top point to preside over his ritual of passing
through the portal. The priest now walks around the circle
with his candle in his receptive hand and enters the center
of the circle from the bottom two points and speaks...

*"I enter the circle of life and magick, to renew
myself as a spiritual Satyr of the Otherkin! I walk
the path of the satyrs within this life in spirit and
honor those spirits that guide me. Let me remain
again in this year as the Satyr that resides within
my soul and continue upon my path. Hail Thee!!"*

The priestess standing outside the circle now lights his
candle from hers and places the crystal tip of the wand
upon his forehead to grant her blessing. He now steps
through the top point of the grid and moves to stand by
her side. The other members of the coven now begin to
step through the circle one at a time and speak their place
as Otherkin then have their candles lit and be granted
blessing by the priest and/or priestess. When all members
have completed the passing through the portal of magick,
the rite continues.

With all members having passed through the portal, each member starting with the clergy of the coven, now begins to place their candle within the circle near the crystals if possible. When all candles are placed inside the circle, each member of the coven makes offerings to the spirits of nature. Offerings may be placed within the circle near the members candle if possible. The priest/ess or shaman of the coven now stands and speaks as the drumbeat begins again...

> *"We make our offerings this day, to celebrate the Earth and sun. We ask the spirits for their guidance and wisdom upon this path of the Otherkin. We feel in our hearts that we are not as human as would appear on the outside and we ask the spirits to honor us with their blessing. Grant your blessing upon this coven of Otherkin and grant us guidance in our days to come. Let us rejoice in the spring and fertility of life!"*

The drums get louder as the participants dance to raise energy in the morning sun. At this time the shaman or priest/ess may perform other blessing and empowerment rites for the coven. When all are ready, the ritual may be closed being sure to gather the crystals and any leftover candle wax from the area.

Chapter Six
April – Seed Moon & Beltane

The coming of April heralds the time to plant the seeds of magick and fill the heart and home with the joy of light and life. The month of April often brings the rains needed to stimulate growth in the earth and fertility is reaching for its peak. The full moon of April is called the *"Seed Moon,"* as this is the time that the seeds planted in March, have begun to sprout. By this time of year, the frost has mostly gone away and the Earth is in bloom. Whether you have planted physical seeds for vegetables and plants or spiritual seeds for growth in the year to come, April is a time of growth, magick and joy for the Otherkin coven.

The celebration of Beltane is also on the 30th of April or 1st of May and is a powerful time of magick amongst covens. The Wiccan tradition sees this time of year as the marriage of the Goddess and God but traditional witches are said to fly to the witch's sabbat on Beltane and/or Midsummer, to meet the black man and learn more of the art of magick. Beltane and Midsummer are both classic times of fairy magick and revelry, considered *"evil"* by the masses. While the hours of night are shorter, the warmth of the season allows for more in the way of nude rites and working magick into the wee hours of the morning.

"Planting the seeds of magick," on the Seed Moon in this month can be representative of many things. This can be for long-term effects in spells and rituals, initiations,

casting influence magick, and working with new spirits, be they fairy, daemon or *"Other."* With the fertility of the Earth during this time of year, spells or rituals that are performed on or during the Seed Moon for financial gains, new friendships, relationships, etc, will grow with the fertility that is accessed during April. This is a time of allowing the abundance of the earth and fertility into your life in any and all the aspects that you can. Nurture any plans that you have set in motion in the growing Spring and watch them come to fruition and flourish during the later parts of the year. Remember that what we grow during Spring, will give us nourishment and be ready to harvest by the end of the year. So if we plan and plant carefully, providing the nourishment that our creations need and remove the weeds that impede its growth, it will be a source of abundance in our lives for many years to come. Plant the perennials now for your future and enjoy the fertility and love in Spring.

Otherkin Initiation Rite

This rite is composed with the information in mind from coven *"Initiations"* in Chapter One. Initiation rites are not just about the acceptance of a new member into the coven, but are about the new person's attainment and use of new knowledge within the coven and within their own life. This rite is to be performed when a member of the coven has shown growth within themselves and their use of magical and spiritual practices. This could be thought of as admittance to the next level and recognition of the accomplishments of the individual rather than an initiation. These rituals are representative of the growth attained and can help the initiate to realize that they have grown on their path and can give them the push they need to continue. The next step for the individual is dependent on the coven and the individual's desire for learning other aspects of their craft.

There are many components to be considered before giving this ritual to someone and the rite can be changed as necessary for the needs of each coven and individual. Components to consider are ...

In what aspect(s) of the craft has the initiate shown growth and/or mastery? This may be in some healing modality, spellcraft, divination, empowerment rites, shamanic practices, overall wisdom in council of others etc...

Does the coven feel that the initiate has attained a greater state of ability with that practice? You will have to ask each member to give his or her Honest Opinion!!

Does the initiate use this ability with wisdom and grace? This means that they are willing to work with anyone within the coven or outside as necessary.

Is the initiate expanding into other practices successfully? Expansion is the key to honoring our inner spirit. You may not be aware of what other interests that they have, so be sure to ask them if you need to.

Does the initiate honor the path of Otherkin that they walk? In other words, if they are a wolf, elf, satyr, nymph, dragon, etc, do they work with abilities and practices that align them with that inner Otherkin spirit? You may need to ask their viewpoint on the matter.

Does the initiate feel that they are ready to honor themselves in having and using this ability and move forward by accepting the ritual? This is entirely the initiate's choice.

This list of questions can go on but we should not make it too complicated to achieve an initiation ritual for the growth and acceptance of coven members. The following ritual is based from a mild ordeal rite that was mentioned earlier in this book and in the author's first work, *"The Book of Satyr Magick."* The *"Naked & Alone Ordeal Rite,"* is used here with some minor additions to represent the growth of the member and their abilities on the path. Items used for this rite can and will change among groups, what is written here is a basic to get you started and give an understanding of the symbolism used in the rite.

Items: Lantern (for wisdom)
    A book (for knowledge)
    Crystal (for healing)
    Herbs (for herbal craft)
    Candle (for spellcraft)
    Drum (for shamanic abilities)
    Small Mirror (for divination)

This list is representative of the abilities attained and may need more items for other abilities representations. To begin the ritual, have a place in a forest that can be used for the initiation rite. Find a path that is fairly well known, but at a time of day such as nearing twilight, that no one else will be in the area outside of coven members. Without the initiate knowing, secretly take the items that best represent the abilities of the initiate and walk the path to a place that they can be left for the initiate to *"find."* This can be on a particular rock or near a certain tree, etc. The initiate prepares by meditating for a period of time before the rite begins and when all is in place, the initiate must disrobe (if possible, use caution and common sense) and be told what path to walk until they find the items left by the coven members. The initiate must walk, nude to the place that the items are left and upon finding them, spend some time in contemplation over what the items mean. After a short period of time in contemplation, the initiate will carry the items back to the coven members and reveal what they have discovered in contemplation over the items. The coven may wish to have a gift such as a new cloak, etc, waiting secretly for the initiate to congratulate and honor them as a person that has grown upon their path and helps others in the process.

The purpose of this rite is to first, give the initiate a challenge in walking nude to an unknown location and find an unknown object(s) that requires them to think about its meaning. They may have an overall understanding of the meaning to the object, but need to consider what it represents to them and apply this to the path that they walk. The second purpose here is to aid the initiate in understanding what they have achieved through the use of this ability and be able to feel a moment at least of pride in themselves for doing what they do and being who they are.

So let me break down the representations. The initiate begins nude and walking into the forest alone. They return to you and have retrieved a lantern, which they have lit, a book and a crystal that the coven members planted at a prearranged location in the forest. Now the representation here is that the initiate first arrived to the coven, nude, (honest without anything to hide), and over time (walking in the forest and returning) have discovered/attained their abilities with wisdom (lighted lantern) knowledge (the book) and healing practices (the crystal). This person spent some time in the forest that allowed them to consider what these items mean and return after attaining a realization. This may also be a time in which the spirits of the forest plant new ideas in the mind of the initiate if they are able to reach a deep enough state of meditation and contemplation in the forest alone. This is the reason for the sharing what they experienced with the members of the coven upon return.

As you can see, the symbolism of the ritual is very deep and should be considered when sending an initiate into the forest or when walking nude into the forest yourself.

Seed Moon Ritual

As the Seed Moon is a time of growing abundance and prosperity for the Earth, this may also be a good time for the coven to gather for rites of abundance and prosperity as well. As mentioned in the first chapter of this book, this can be a time of gathering for *"needed magic,"* amongst the coven and combining this special time with the *"planting the seeds of magick,"* in April will aid the coven members in the months to come.

Before beginning some basic ritual for abundance, consider the abilities of the coven members, individually and as a whole. Consider the ways in which the coven can attain a greater financial state and grow together in the mean time. I know that many people will have busy schedules with jobs, school, kids, parents, etc, in today's world but we often add things to our lives that are not necessary, they are just our routines. In looking at the routines amongst members, we have to consider what things are in the way and really necessary and which ones truly add to our growth as a spiritual being. For example, the average person will say that they do not have time to learn and practice meditation. This is a prime example because these are usually people that will spend more time on their phones, texts, ipads, watching TV, etc, not realizing that they are wasting a big part of their spiritual life and ability while claiming this thing to be important. It only takes a total of twenty minutes a day for meditation practice, and they will spend every hour they can, creating some excuse not to learn. So once we determine what may be in the way and needs changing in our lives we can determine what abilities we have to create greater financial gain as individuals and with the whole of the coven.

The following ritual combines the lunar ritual with chakra healing work for the coven. This may be done by a fire or by candle light as needed. You may wish to have each member of the coven consider what plants or items best represent money and finance to them. Finding the mental connection to represent "money" in magic is very important and it may take a few tries to find your proper money herb or item.

Need: Carnelian stone (one for each member)
    Five Orange candles (or campfire)
    Flour or stones
    Rattle
    Drum & beater
    Live potted herbs or items
      (For abundance/wealth)

Create a circle of flour or stones on the ground or floor. You may also wish to create a pentagram in the circle with flour. Place the five orange candles at each of the points of the pentagram and have all attendants be seated around the circle. Each member of the coven will need to have his or her piece of carnelian held in their receptive hand in their lap or nearest to the sacral or navel chakra. They may hold a mudra with this hand such as the cosmic mudra, with the first finger and thumb lightly touching and the rest of the fingers relaxed and pointing outwards if they wish or simply allow the hand to relax and hold the stone. The mudra may help the carnelian stone to channel more energy to the chakra center for this rite. Potted plants or items that represent abundance and wealth may be placed in between the candles at the points of the pentagram or simply in front of each member, again to increase the energy flow. Now the priest/ess or shaman of the coven, stands with the rattle and moves behind the coven members while casting the circle to include them in the energy. When the circle is cast the priest/ess or shaman will move to a place at the top point of the circle and begin the rite.

A drumbeat gently begins as the priest/ess or shaman speaks...

"Upon this night, we gather to honor the Seed Moon, as a time of growth and abundance upon the Earth. By the powers of the fertility spirits, may we grow to become more successful in our lives and to see the ways in which we can grow and contribute to the world around us. We all know that the spirit world is not one of money and finances. Yet we must live in both worlds and tend to our spiritual life as well as our physical one. Upon this night we call to the spirits from between the worlds, to guide us to understand what holds us back from accomplishing the lives that we seek upon this Earth. Spirits, by the power of the drum, may we journey within our souls

and minds tonight, to learn what blocks our path and find the ways of creating in our world, to mimic the ways of the spirits of the Moon. By the carnelian stones let us open to the grand Emperor or Empress in our lives and create a world of joy and abundance from within."

The priest/ess or shaman begins a gentle shamanic chanting as the drumbeat continues and the coven members begin to chant while focusing on the carnelian stones in their hand…

Coven's Chant: "I awaken the Emperor/ Empress of my life."

As the coven members chant, the drumbeat grows louder and faster. Each member of the coven begins to visualize themselves being bathed in bright orange light as they journey deeper into their consciousness. In this journey, each member should be asking questions about their ability to earn money or attain financial gain in the physical world. If they can at this time, they may contact a guide or power animal to take them to where they need to be and show them or teach them what they need to learn. This may take some time, so the drummer needs to be capable of continuing and knowing how to perform a call back when the rite is about to end. Using a call back with the drum, means that the beat will stop, then beat many times very fast and stop again briefly, then continue to drum until all members of the coven have opened their eyes to signify their return.

A group journey such as this can be very empowering to all members of the coven as it gives them a sense of journeying together and yet for them selves to attain what they seek. Using the stones will aid in opening the sacral chakra to boost the journeywork and help them to connect with a spirit that can guide them in the ways of money and finances.

When all have come back from the journey, the priest/ess or shaman will give thanks to the spirits for their guidance and wisdom and then close the circle. The members of the coven may wish to share their experiences to help in determining symbolism "*seen,*" within the journey and to understand any teachings that they were given. If they need it, the shaman or priest/ess of the group can journey for them at a different time to retrieve more information about their path to attaining financial freedom, help in removing blocks and guide them walking the path intended for them.

Beltane Sabbat Journey

The ritual of Beltane is usually celebrated on April 30th or May 1st depending on the tradition. This festival in honor of the approaching summer months is also known as Walpurgis Night in Germany and Germanic countries. This was the time when the witches were said to fly to Brocken's Peak to dance and revel with the Black Man, i.e., the devil of the witch's sabbat.

In honoring the ancient sabbat tradition, this rite is for a shamanic journey amongst the coven to fly to the sabbat on Beltane and connect with the ancient craft of the traditional shamanic witch. While I realize that the traditional witches used what is known today as the *"witches flying ointment"* and it is well known that this ointment was composed of highly toxic and narcotic substances such as deadly nightshade, henbane, black hellebore, poison hemlock, and wolf's bane. This toxic blend of herbs rapidly caused out-of-body experiences and forced the witch into astral projection, so that the ascent to the astral sabbat was made possible. By using the method of astral projection through shamanic journey, the astral sabbat is still made possible, without the threat of using toxic substances.

It will take some preparation among the group that plans to journey to the sabbat and using the weeks prior to Beltane to meditate and prepare the mind is highly suggested. A full blown astral projection experience requires full clarity of mind and focus of thought, or should I say, *"focus of no-thought."* Full projection is achieved when the heart chakra is fully open and compassion flows from the individual. This is a highly enlightened state of being to reach and using the shamanic drumming will give the inertia needed to project to where ever the individual wishes to go. Of course in today's world, CD's and music programs are available to aid the practitioner in achieving deeper states of meditation, such as Steven Halpern's music on the CD, *"Deep Theta."* This is one that I have used many times myself with great results. Simply meditate with the music playing and clear your mind completely. You will have experiences that are far greater in spiritual scope than normal meditation. It may also be suggested to use mantras during the preparation phases before the journey, as this will encourage and train the mind to work with the practitioner's desires for an out-of-body experience.

Also study as much as you can about the astral sabbat in the weeks prior to the ritual, as this will give you a good visual impression of the celebration and an understanding of what to expect. This will aid you in the initial visualization process to further aid the journey. All participants should clear their mind and meditate to open the heart before beginning the rite.

Need: Broom for each member
   Flour or stones
   Five red candles
   Drum & beater
   Rattle
   Blankets to lie on
   Medicine Shield (if available)

To prepare the area, create a circle of flour or stones and mark a pentagram in the center, placing a red candle at each point of the pentagram. The medicine shield of the coven should hang on a wall in front of the top point of the pentagram. Participants in the rite should have a blanket to lie on and a broom beside them. The broom is to encourage the traditional visualization and give the practitioner a tool to fly on. The priest/ess or shaman rattles the circle to clear unwanted energy and cast the circle while chanting. During this time the coven members should continue to clear their minds and focus on the goal. When the circle is cast, the candles should be lit as the drumming starts and the rite begins.

The priest/ess or shaman sits near the top point of the pentagram with the medicine shield behind them and speaks...

> *"We gather this Beltane's eve to journey to the astral sabbat. By the powers of the Moon and Earth, may we walk between worlds and fly unto the ritual celebration. Let the spirits hear us and be as our guides unto the sabbat we fly this night."*

The drumming picks up a faster, steady beat to signal time for the shamanic journey to begin. Each member of the coven gently lays their hand upon the broom at their side, and begins to visualize being in the room or area they are in, while looking at the ritual participants upon the floor. Gently walk around this room in the astral for a moment to get your bearing on being in the astral realm. You may visualize the other members standing up spiritually, while their bodies still lie upon the blankets. Move about in this area for a little bit then lift your broom and will yourself to journey through the ceiling of the room and out into the night sky. Visualize flying off the roof of the house or flying up through the trees and above the treetops. Let your self fly into the night and let the spirit guide you. If you have a spirit guide, you may call upon them and ask them to guide you to the sabbat ritual. The spirit will take you to a place that is usually in the forest or near a river or lake. The bonfires burn to light your way in but be careful of who or what you speak to on your first journey here. Some spirits can mislead you and trick you into things that you would not want to do at first. On the good side of the astral sabbat, you can shapeshift at will, fly, practice vampirism or do anything that you would wish. If you can call upon a particular spirit, they can teach you more in the ways of magic and spiritual practices in this realm. The black man, Satan, or central "*devil figure*" of the sabbat is usually very friendly and will help you in many different ways as far as teaching and understanding from a deeper perspective about the truth of Luciferian spiritual life and being. Listen to these spirits and work with them cautiously and you will reap the benefits of journeying to the astral sabbat, time and time again. Listen for the drumming to call you back and share your experiences with others of the Otherkin coven. Let the priest/ess or shaman close the circle, and give thanks to all the spirits who helped anyone in the coven while journeying to the astral sabbat.

I give precautions in this journey as the sabbat is an open aired place for spirits to gather and there is no "bouncer at the door," to keep out trouble makers. Be careful and if any among the group feel in any way threatened during the sabbat journey, you may simply open your eyes to return to the normal world. This is also the reasoning for the deep meditation practice, as the open heart will repel beings that are malicious or threatening to you. The rule of *"like attracts like,"* is a major point in the astral sabbat to consider. If you are fearful of the journey or have reserves as to what will happen, just don't do it until you can clear your consciousness and release the fears. Remember like attracts like here, holding fears in our hearts will bring out fears in our spiritual journeys. Be careful of your spirit journeys and you will reap the benefits.

Chapter Seven
May – Hare Moon

The coming of the summer months heralds a time of freedom, sensuality, and showing our love of life and nature. The Hare Moon of May is the time to renew your sensuality and ignite the sparks of romance. Celebrate life and love in this month and give your self permission to free your inner wild nature. For the Otherkin coven or practitioner, this gives us permission to follow who we are and allow ourselves to claim our path in the outer world as well as the inner. By celebrating sensuality and pleasure, we confirm our life and existence on Earth. This is an important part of growth that needs to be nurtured and understood even amongst the Otherkin. With the Hare or rabbit as the totem of this month, we can learn much in the ways of being true to our nature, whether we are a predator or prey. Remember that the rabbit is a totem that is connected to the lunar cycles and can take us into the fairy realm when we open our heart to the world around us.

On our journey through the wheel of the year, we should have reached a point of seeing the strong outward growth of our projects in life by now. The seedlings or projects that we contemplated in January, and then started the roots, letting them grow stronger in February and March, should be coming into full bloom and strong development by this time of year. The coming of summer is the height of the growing season and will be reflected in the outward appearance of our project(s). If we need it, we can add greater nourishment to this aspect of our life and aid its continuing growth until the harvest season begins. Remember that it is about what we grow in our life that will make the difference, so grow something that is long-term in its use to aid you in the future. This will create a cycle of abundance in your life later.

As suggested earlier, rituals for the Hare Moon may be created to honor the totem of the rabbit, as a sign of fertility and abundance, as well as a prey animal that gives nourishment to those that would feed upon it. This is also a time for the Green Man to be in fruition and all gods and goddesses of the hunt can be honored in this moon cycle as well. For those feeling a need to reclaim their sensual aspects, working with rituals of kundalini massage or other healing and empowerment rites can be utilized especially at this time of year.

The following ritual is created to honor the wild spirits of nature, mostly as the satyrs and nymphs of the forest, but can be arranged to honor other spirits as needed. Remember that the satyr is a wild pro-creative spirit that embodies many different traits and powers and the nymphs are wise and wild women of the woods and water. The satyrs and nymphs can be very beneficial spirits to work with on the Otherkin path and can guide us to finding our own fertility and abundance, as well as healing, gifts of prophecy, musical teaching, shapeshifting and many other magical abilities. For the purposes of this ritual, the males of the group are satyrs, while the females are the nymphs. This is not necessarily intended to re-enact scenes from classic images of satyr's and nymphs in art and literature but could have a certain amount of play and chasing involved amongst the coven. If at all possible, try to go for a swim before or after the ritual, as a part of enjoying the flesh and loving life in this lunar month's cycle. But keep in mind that the nymphs and satyrs can be considered at times volatile spirits, so be careful not to anger them, lest you incur their wrath.

Satyr's & Nymph's Rite

This rite is best performed in a forest near a natural water source such as lake or river or in a field at the edge of the forest. This ritual can also be performed before sunset in the late afternoon or early evening, if at all possible. This invokes the lighter side of these spirits of the forest, so that the energy will be easier to work with and handle as the night comes forth. You may wish to work nude or scantily clad for the best results. The coven members that deem themselves a bit poetic may wish to recite or improvise some forest or nature based poetry that seems fitting for the occasion.

Need: Musical instruments
(Drums, flutes, rattles, tambourines etc)
Fire pit or campfire
Offerings of wine
(Or small amounts of liquor, honey, and flowers such as orchids, roses, thyme, rosemary etc,)

This is a less structured ritual of enticing the spirits as well as a minor possession rite to let the spirits come through you. Begin the rite by building a fire in a pit or build a campfire surrounded with stones from the area. Once the fire is burning, the priest/ess or shaman of the coven will begin the rite...

> *"Upon this eve, we gather here to call to the spirits of the forest. Spirits of forest and field come forth and let us feel your presence. Dance with us to our music, or come into us and teach us your songs. We open ourselves to the ways of the spirits, satyrs and nymphs. Ride within us and grant us your blessings! Accept our offerings from humble hearts, our music from humble hands and our poetry from humble minds. May we be blessed in this rite, begin!"*

Each member of the coven places their offering to the spirits, satyrs or nymphs, near the fire and a soft music begins to be heard from the flutes. Let each member take a moment to listen to this soft melody to open the heart and clear the mind of excessive thoughts. This will allow for the music to flow from those playing an instrument, or poetry to flow from those that wish to recite or improvise a poem.

After a few minutes of listening to the flute, other members may join in the music or dance to their hearts delight. Allow times in between songs to be available for those who wish to recite poems or improvise. You may wish to make a friendly challenge of it to see who the best poet is amongst the group. Allow this to feel like a full celebration of life and joy instead of like a ritual so that you can feel the happiness flowing through the group. This ritual can go on for hours into the night as you wish or have available. If anyone of the coven begins to show signs of possession, keep an eye on them to be sure that they have an easy transfer back to normal consciousness.

Signs of possession can be many different things. The "*duende*" that takes over dancers and musicians can make them able to play or dance in ways that they could not ordinarily perform. Poets, who get "*inspired*" i.e., in spirit, can make poems last for long periods of time and they will make perfect sense by the end of the poem. Other signs of possession can be in the form of speaking in an unknown language or seeming to be disoriented about where they are as well as claiming to be someone else, such as a deity or particular spirit. These things don't happen as often as the TV would have us believe but never the less they do happen. The purpose of this open aired ritual is to remind us that the spirits are here, without excessive trappings and needs for ritual decorations, adornments, or motions. They are free flowing energies that will be attracted to the sound and rhythm of the music we make. I have been taken by the duende playing guitars, drumming and dancing at many different times in my life and have had a wonderful time working with this energy. I have also found that for myself, I can feel the satyr's energy easily while playing a pan flute and banging a tambourine against my legs and staggering out a circle dance around the area. This is without any circle preparations or casting corners etc. The spirits are available but we may be blocking them with excess ritual regalia. Allow this rite to let you be free, as is according to the moon phase of May.

When the ritual has ended, you should let each member give their thanks to any spirits felt through the course of the rite and be sure not to leave any thing behind if you are camping or in the forest.

Hare Moon Journey

This ritual is a shamanic journey for the full moon to spiritually *"follow the rabbit down the hole"* and go into the Otherworld to speak to the Green Man, Pan, Cernunnos, etc. In this way, we are honoring the rabbit spirit as a guide to the faery realm and as a spirit of fertility and abundance.

Need: Flour or stones
    Seven green candles
    Drum & beater
    Rattle
    Wand
    Flowers and plants as Offerings and décor
    Blankets or pillows to sit or lie on
    Medicine Shield (if available)
    Statues of Pan, the Green Man, or Cernunnos
    Journals (for notes after the journey)

To begin this rite, cast a large circle of flour or stones to mark the area. Make sure that it is large enough for all ritual participants to sit or lie within. The priest/ess or shaman of the group will rattle the circle to clear away unwanted energy and use the wand to cast the circle...

> *"I cast thee sacred circle of power*
> *Focused here, from this hour!"*

After the circle is cast, place the candles around the circle in a septagram pattern and use the wand to activate the grid. Place the coven Medicine shield at or near the top point of the septagram for all members to see. You may place the statues of the deities around the circle to give each member of the coven a good representation of the spirit they are journeying to speak to. Now the priest/ess or shaman of the group will light the candles and be seated near the center of the circle with the drum and beater close by. The shaman or priest/ess of the coven will begin the rite...

> *"We gather this night of the Hare Moon to journey to the Otherworld, and honor the rabbit as a totem, of our craft and spirit of fertility. Let all who gather in this circle join into the journey of the spirit and let us each communicate with the Green Man of the forest. Let us find Pan or Cernunnos in the Otherworld, and we ask them for their guidance and wisdom, to teach us about the ways of the rabbit, and all the spirits of*

fertility and abundance. Great spirits, teach us this night the lessons we most need to learn about how to walk in balance on the Earth, and show us how we can move forward in our lives. Hail Thee Cernunnos! Hail Thee Pan! Hail Thee Green Man of the forest!"

The coven calls back... "Hail Thee Cernunnos! Hail Thee Pan! Hail Thee Green Man of the forest!"

The drumbeat begins slowly as all participants place their offerings near the candles within the circle. The priest/ess or shaman of the coven will raise their hands to the air above them and speak again...

"We offer unto thee, our gifts from the forest and ask that you accept these humble offerings, as a token of our gratitude and thanks for the lives we have. Grant us your guidance upon this night of the Hare Moon and let us follow the Hare into the Otherworld! Hail Thee!!"

The coven again calls, "Hail Thee!"

The drumbeat speeds up as the journey begins. The shaman or priest/ess of the coven will chant and rattle for a time during the beginning of the rite to aid all members in attaining journey consciousness. Each member of the group should go to their place in the astral plane and see the rabbit spirit coming towards them. Often this spirit will act as it would in the physical plane and upon realizing that it is seen, will dart away from the person before them. At this point, the coven members should follow the rabbit until they get to its hole or follow it into the bushes. When the rabbit goes down the hole in the astral plane, you will squeeze your self down the hole after it. You will emerge in the Middle world and you may see Pan, Cernunnos, or the Green Man, standing before you, or perhaps sitting on a wooden throne in the forest. He may or may not appear as you are used to seeing so be prepared if he is not what you expect. He can be intimidating and at times frightening to see. Remember what you wanted to ask him about your physical life, abundance, fertility, etc., and listen carefully to what he has to tell you. Spend some time conversing with this wise being of the Earth and pay close attention to everything he says. When the call back begins on the drum, you should thank Him for any information that he has given you and bid him farewell. You may chose to go back through the rabbit hole or take another way back to your place in the astral before returning to normal consciousness. As soon as you return to normal consciousness, lift your journal and write down everything you can from the journey being sure to write anything that you were told in answers to your questions or things that the Green Man may have suggested to you about your life in the physical. When all members of the coven have returned to normal consciousness, the priest/ess or shaman of the group will begin to close the circle. Each member should give thanks for their journey and any information that they received from the Otherworld. Spend some time talking amongst yourselves, sharing your stories about what you experienced while talking to the Lord of the Forest. Be sure to look for any signs that they may have warned you about and follow up on any advice you were given, as it may change your life forever.

Chapter Eight
June – Dyad Moon & Summer Solstice

The month of June brings us to the height of the growing season and the sun's brightest point during the year. Everything after June is a decline for the power of the sun and a rising of power for the Moon and darkness. The Dyad Moon is a time to confirm and affirm your growth or the growth of your projects in life. By this time of year, the old has been removed and the new is in full swing of growth and health. The full moon of June is a time to seek new adventure or enjoy the fruits of the adventure you are currently undertaking. It is rather funny that our society has made June the first month of summer from school days, as this falls directly into the time of seeking new adventure on the lunar calendar. This is also the month of many summer vacations whether we are still in school or not.

The name of the Dyad Moon is very special for the Otherkin because it literally translates as *"two-ness,"* or *"otherness,"* representing the otherworld of spirit combined with the physical world of flesh. Dyad was once the title used by Pythagoreans for the number two, while the name given to the number one or in religious terms, *"god"* was *"monad."* We still see the use of part of this terminology in the word, *"mono,"* which still means one.

The Summer Solstice is considered a special time for magick amongst all traditions. This is a time for the fairy folk to dance in the moonlight and play tricks upon unwary travelers or innocent victims. As I mentioned in chapter 6, the rites of Beltane and the Summer Solstice are conventional times for traditional witches to fly to the astral sabbat, to revel in congress with other spirits and daemons that cavort there. For those that wish, this may be an option for your coven gathering at this time of year. The summer solstice also begins the cycle of lunar power, represented by the beginning of the sign of Cancer, the Crab. This makes this solstice celebration one of the most important for all practitioners of magick.

For those who wish to contact the fae folk, you may wish to begin by working with the forest or woodland spirits, such as the dryads and hamadryads, during the summer months. For those who are not sure, the dryads are woodland spirits in general, while hamadryads are tree spirits that will die with the tree. Remember that some stories tell of witches that looked like trees from behind so this makes a strong connection for the Otherkin practitioners or any witches that work with tree spirits. Performing meditations in the forest as a coven can help in connecting and communicating with the forest and tree spirits as well. You may wish to bring offerings of water and fresh soil to place around the tree, aiding its growth and health in coming years as an offering in trade for communication. Any plants that are brought to the area should be carefully treated when picked so that you encourage the spirits communication with you and your group.

For the Otherkin that are not as interested in trees as in daemons, there is also a collection of spirits in the grimoires that are considered to be forest dwelling wanderers. These mostly come from the *"Ars Theurgia"* and may all be qualified as spirits of the air as well as dryads of the forest, not owing to any cardinal direction.

Betel -- docile spirit summoned in the forest, teaches the wisdom of Adam and the virtues of the Creator.

Emoniel – wandering prince of the forests and woodlands. As a spirit of the air, he may be made more visible after summoning him by use of a scrying crystal.

Nasiniet – servant of prince Emoniel, has a fondness of forests and woodlands

Ennoniel – one of the chief servants of Emoniel that is drawn to woodland areas

Edriel – one of twelve dukes in service of Emoniel, can manifest by day or night

Dramiel – another duke who serves Emoniel

Hydriel – a wandering prince who has a great love of the water, and may be more apt to manifest in swamps or bogs.

Dusiriel – one of twelve dukes who serve the infernal wandering prince Hydriel, prefers to appear in swamps or wetlands, may appear in a naga form

This gives you eight different spirits and will conclude this list of daemons that can be called upon from any forest areas. I will mention that all of these spirits are said to have a good nature and each has a host of lesser spirits that serve them. We should keep in mind that the word daemon originally meant nature spirit and this might be a better way to call upon the faery spirits by name.

Dyad Moon Ritual

Before beginning the rite of the Dyad Moon, the members of the Otherkin coven may wish to spend some time considering what growth has occurred in their lives by this time of year. Look back over previous months and see what stages your life or projects were in at the beginning of the year and how much has changed over the course of the last six months or so. Allow yourself to see the path rather than getting caught up in the unpleasant details. All paths lead somewhere and each must be walked one step at a time. After you have given yourself ample time to think over your path, affirm to yourself out loud that this has really happened and that you can see how things have unfolded for you in the last six months. This is an important part of "following the moon," as the confirmation and affirmation of growth will encourage you to continue. We all want everything to be instantaneous in growth and change, but we need to reconnect with the Earth and Moon to understand how life *really* works. That way being slowly and one step at a time.

The rite of the Dyad Moon is a ritual of balancing our dual nature and embracing the *"Other,"* as stated earlier in this section.

Need: Flour or stones
    Offerings for spirits of place etc.
    3 Black candles
    3 White candles
    1 Red candle
    Medicine shield
    Rattle
    Drum & Beater

Create a circle of flour or stones on the ground or floor to mark the area. Place the three white candles to the eastern side of the circle and the three black candles to the western side of the circle. This should basically make a sideways hexagram within the circle. The points in this grid will face east and west rather than north to south as in traditional drawings. (See below) Finally place the red candle in the center, symbolizing the life force that is created from light and shadow. The medicine shield may be placed at the northern most point of the circle on a stand or hanging on a wall or tree depending on where you are.

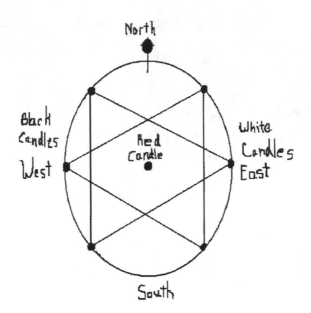

The priest/ess or shaman of the coven will cast the circle with the rattle and light the candles, beginning with the white candles first then, moving clockwise from the northeast, around the circle until all six candles are lit. The red candle in the center is lit last. The priest/ess or shaman then moves to stand at the northern most point near the medicine shield and speaks...

> *"Upon this night of the Dyad Moon, we gather to recognize our own growth in this life, and seek to walk in balance of shadow and light. May we all find our inner peace and understand that growth is important in our world, both for the spirit, and the body. Let us be blessed upon this night, as we stand between the worlds, and see our selves as a whole and as a part of this creation!"*

The drumbeat begins as the shaman or priest/ess moves to the southern point of the circle. He or she stands for a moment in silence, clearing their mind and focusing their energy and then steps over the boundary of the circle and stands near the center where the red candle illuminates the circle. He or she opens their arms and speaks aloud…

"As I walk within the circle of life, I gain wisdom of balance between light and shadow. Within the world of man, and within the world of the spirit, I recognize myself as the consciousness within this body, the spirit that controls its own destiny, capable of great good or great harm. I balance my soul and body within this circle of light and life and step forth into the world again. May I be blessed as I pass through the circle once again."

The priest/ess or shaman steps through the northern point of the circle and turns to stand near the medicine shield. Now other members of the coven will pass through the circle, and speak in their own words, of what they feel this circle represents to their life and path. Each member is encouraged to see the balance of light and shadow within the world and to confirm their own life and reasons for being. The priest/ess or shaman will stand to bless and welcome them as they pass back through the circle into the ordinary world.

After each member of the coven has passed through the circle, the coven may chose to move into shapeshifting rites or any rituals that embrace balance and the *"other,"* that may be a part of this gathering. Offerings should be left for the spirits and thanks given to them when all is complete. The priest/ess or shaman may close the circle and allow the candles to burn out.

Summer Solstice Ritual

The rite for the Summer Solstice is a time of power, both of the sun reaching its height and in the exchange of power with the moon. For the Otherkin coven, this can be a time of intensive ritual working, using the powers of the sun and moon, connecting to the spirits and daemons of the forest, journeying to the faery realms and connecting with the tree and plant spirits in nature. For those that want to work with the daemons of the forest as mentioned earlier, the evocations used here can be changed to suit your needs. You may also need to journey to speak to the daemon(s) prior to the ritual for the solstice to attain a sigil for the rite of evocation. This sigil can be drawn upon the ground or floor within the circle during the ritual casting. The following ritual is best performed out doors and can be performed in the afternoon, when the sun is still high in the sky if you wish. This is a Middle world journey to the place that you are physically located, to commune with the tree spirits around you.

Need: Drum & beater
   Flour or stones
   Rattle

Offerings for the spirits
   (Water for the trees?)
Small scrying crystal (if needed)
Five green candles
Smudge wand & shell or bowl
Wand or Staff
Medicine shield
Feather fan (if available)
Journal for notes after the journey

Begin the rite by creating a circle of flour or stones on the ground or floor, big enough for all members to sit around the outer edge. If you are intending to summon a particular spirit, you will want to draw their sigil within the circle at this time. Place the five green candles within the circle to form a pentagram with the top pointing north and place the offerings for the spirits within the middle of the pentagram. The medicine shield may hang above the top point of the pentagram or be placed on a stand within the circle at this point. The priest/ess or shaman of the group will begin by igniting the smudge wand and cleansing all members of the coven starting with their self, then begin to cleanse the space for the circle to be activated. Walking clockwise around the circle, the priest/ess or shaman smudges the area, wafting the smoke with their hand or feather fan to create this sacred space. Now the shaman or priest/ess picks up the wand or staff to activate the pentagram grid within the circle before lighting the candles. Once the candles are lit, they take their place at the northern point of the pentagram and speak...

> *"By the powers of the Summer Solstice, we gather here today, to commune with the spirits of the trees. By the powers of the sun and moon may we journey to the Middle world, to stand within this place in the spirit realm and attain guidance and wisdom from the forest spirits. Spirits of the forest, accept our offerings unto the Earth and trees, and guide us to your wisdom upon this day."*

A slow drumbeat begins as the ritual attendants are seated around the outer edge of the circle. The circle here is a portal for the group to use to get into the Otherworld. If you have a spirit or daemon sigil drawn within the circle, it is a place of power for the spirit to manifest and you may need to pass the scrying crystal around after you have evoked the spirit for members to see it. All members that are taking the journey should spend a moment in clearing their mind and centering themselves before the full journey begins. The shaman or priest/ess speaks again...

> *"Spirits of the Earth and Air, we evoke thee to this place, to commune with us and grant us your wisdom and guidance. By the power of the sun and moon, come forth to speak with us and let us attain your knowledge and wisdom of this life and world. Hail thee!!"*

The drumbeat gets faster as the ritual attendants relax into the journey. For this journey, members of the coven will want to visualize the place that they are at in the physical world in their minds as their entrance point to the Otherworld. When you can see your surroundings clearly in your mind, then look about you and see what spirits or beings are making themselves known to you. Look to the trees and ask if any of them will share their knowledge or wisdom with you about certain subjects that concern you or an area of your life that you need assistance in. You may also simply ask them to speak to you and ask them how they are doing. If you have summoned a particular spirit or daemon of the forest, look in the circle above the sigil and they may be waiting there for you to speak. Pay close attention to how they appear to you as they will often take a form that has a hidden meaning for you. Journey and speak to the spirits within this journey and gain any insights or information that you can and listen for the call back to start. When you hear the callback on the drum, finish up whatever you are doing, and give thanks to the spirit before leaving the Otherworld. When you come back to regular consciousness, write down everything that you can about your journey while waiting for the others of the coven to finish up their journeys. When all have completed their journeys and written down their experience, you may again share stories of what you saw in the Otherworld and compare notes or get information about images etc. When you are ready, the shaman or priest/ess of the coven may close the circle, or move into other ritual works upon the Summer Solstice.

Chapter Nine
July – Mead Moon

The month of July brings us to the Mead Moon and is a time to relax and bask in the summer sun. The lunar month for July is considered a time to take time for the self and may be spent as time to rejuvenate and heal amongst the Otherkin coven. For any projects that we are creating, this is a time of patience and allowing them to continue to grow until we reach harvest time in the next month on the lunar calendar. This can be a time of nourishment and a much needed rest under the summer sun.

For Otherkin coven rituals, we may seek to gather to perform more healing rites or simple and gentle empowerments amongst the group. These should be as relaxing as possible and make each rite to aid the removal of stress and worry from our daily life. For those that are still adventurous and energetic, you may wish to work with some weather magic at this time of year, to try to encourage the rains to continue nourishing the earth before the harvest season begins. This can also be a source of aid to your own growing projects in life.

I know that many people in our society have a difficult time with the concept of relaxation. As a practicing healer, I realize that we have taught ourselves that relaxation requires one to go to sleep or take a nap, but this is not really the case, nor what is intended here. We also tend to think excessively when we are not busy doing something and this again is a product of our society. We believe we must do *too much* and therefore get out of balance more often. Spending time in relaxation can mean many things, but mostly means letting go of the troubles and worries of daily life and spending time with yourself or *truly being yourself* when you are with friends or family. Joking, and having fun, keeping the mood light or doing gentle activities such as listening to relaxing music, exploring and strolling in the forest or taking a relaxing swim in a lake or river, can be just as much a part of relaxation as going to a spa and getting a massage or a mud wrap. The point is the mind frame of not being in a hurry or pushing yourself to achieve a whole lot at a time. Seek a peaceful enjoyment and take some time to relax and unwind in this month and honor the cycle of the Mead Moon.

Otherkin Group Healing Rite

For Otherkin coven rituals, gathering to do a group-healing rite during the time of year for relaxing is perfect for connecting to our inner selves again. For healing work, be creative and improvise some activities for fun, as well as crystal healing sessions or energy work. Gather indoors and paint pictures, play psychotropic or ambient music and make spiritual crafts together, such as Medicine Shields, Dream Catchers or wands and tools for the coven. This is a time for creative magic and you may stir up the energy for a different kind of Otherkin experience, if you use your creative energies and the happiness of the coven.

The following ritual is a rite that invokes and balances the energy of the colors of the rainbow (the chakra centers) and the light and dark energies into the members of the coven. You may wish to time this with the waxing moon of this month to grow in healing and relaxation with this moon cycle. Gather the needed items and begin.

Need: One candle of each color of the rainbow,

(Red, orange, yellow, green, blue, and light & dark purple)

***Note** I have never seen an "indigo" candle for the third eye chakra, so I use the dark and light side of purple to fill in.

One Black candle
One White candle
Flour or stones for circle

To begin, create a circle of flour or stones upon the floor or ground in the center of your area. Draw the septagram (seven pointed star) in the center of the circle and place a candle at each of the points beginning with red at the top point and ending with dark and then light purple. Place the black candle in the center to the left side of the circle and the white candle in the center to the right side of the circle. The priest/ess or shaman of the group will begin lighting the candles from the red at the top point around the circle to the light purple and then light the white and black candles in the center. The coven members may be seated around the circle and take a moment to breathe deeply and focus their minds on the balancing work at hand. Members of the coven should use the brightly colored circle as an aid in visualizing their own chakras and energies. After a moment of silence and peaceful introspection, the priest/ess or shaman speaks.

"Upon this night, under the Mead Moon, we gather here to energize our spirits, and bring our selves back into balance of the darkness and the light. Let us use this time to focus within and bring about healing and rest unto our bodies, minds and spirits. Just as the setting of colored light before us, we too are the rainbow in miniature. Let us energize our chakras and let the powers of light and sound bring us into a state of balance and joy, clear of mind and open in heart."

The priest/ess or shaman begins to hum or intone a sound or mantra such as the sound of *"Aahhh"* or OM. As this sound develops from the depths of his or her being, other around the circle begin to intone in harmony with the priest/ess. The vocal toning begins softly, bringing the members of the coven into a more balanced state and allowing them to intone to strengthen the sound. As the power of the sound resonates through the group, the entire coven is intoning together for healing and relaxation. Allow this powerful sound to envelop the group and carry for as long as possible, or until the group slowly becomes quiet. As the vocal toning settles into silence, take a moment of quiet again before closing the healing circle and extinguish the candles.

Vocal toning can be a very powerful spiritual tool for meditational work or healing and balancing. It does require one to practice and listen carefully to any others that are intoning with you. When practicing vocal toning, allow a moment for your throat and voice to clear in order to get a good tone. It can take a moment to get fluctuations out of the vocal cords and the negative vibrations removed from the body. This type of ritual allows the coven to take time to grow in harmony by practicing vocal toning as a group.

Mead Moon Ritual

The rites of July's Mead Moon should be about relaxation and taking time for the self, to soak up the sun and release our fears and worries. This is a time to heal and rejuvenate before the work of the harvest season begins again in early August. Unfortunately, for many of us, the summer is just as much a time of stress as the rest of the year. Our modern world makes demands that are ongoing and our lives can be full of turmoil all year if we allow them to be. This ritual is for those Otherkin or witches that reside in the modern world and have to deal with the stress of regular life.

Daily stress takes its toll on modern people and can cause a number of physical health problems as well as ruin the life of the individual living under these conditions. This is a simple spell/ritual that can be worked as a coven to either, identify the source of the problem if the person is unaware of it, or help to remove the stressful situation through the spell. By using the group working, each coven member is adding their own energy into the working for each other's benefit, as well as their own. This provides more energy for the spell through the power of the group and the full moon. To begin this rite, gather the needed items under the full moon of July and destroy the blockage from your path.

Need: Cauldron (or large pan on the stove)
Fresh water
2 Red Candles
Ashtray or fireproof container
Smudge wand (cedar or sage)
Brew: rose petals, lavender, chamomile, or any herbs that aid your relaxation
Bluebell flowers (for truth in the matter)
Small pieces of paper
Understanding of cause of your stress; i.e., finances, job, relationships, family, friends, addictions, fears, self-destructive habits, etc.

To begin, the shaman or priest/ess of the group will smudge each member of the coven starting with them selves to cleanse away any energy that may block their ability to relax. Next, begin to build a small campfire or if you can't get out doors, then use the cauldron or a large pan on the stovetop. Set up the red candles and fireproof container near the fire or on a table near by. Fill the cauldron or pan about half full of fresh water, and allow the water to begin to boil. During this time the coven members should focus on the stress that they feel *most blocks them* from relaxing and enjoying themselves. Each member should write what brings them the most stress on the paper or draw an image that best represents this situation in their life. When the water comes to a boil, each member of the coven will take up a small handful of the herbs for relaxation and drop them in the boiling water. For those that need to find the truth of their situation, take a handful of the bluebell flowers and add them to the brew. Allow the steam to build and each member should breathe it in or waft it over them as they gently toss in their handful of herbs, to aid their relaxation and rest. Now the shaman or priest/ess stands before everyone and speaks...

> *"Upon this night, we gather to relax and enjoy ourselves under the Mead Moon. But each of us has things in their life that keep us from this time of rest and enjoyment in the summer nights. So tonight, we seek to identify and remove what blocks us in our life."*

The shaman or priest/ess lights the red candles and speaks again...

> *"By the powers of the full moon, we gain our strength to face this challenge and allow our selves*

rest in this month, from within our spirit and within our lives. Hail thee, Spirits of the Moon!"

The coven calls back...

"Hail thee, Spirits of the Moon!"

The priest/ess or shaman now begins the chant...

Sacred fire
Burning bright
Remove what blocks
Our path this night
Let this stress
Be burned away
Grant us rest
In coming days!

Let the chant build through the coven while each member ignites and burns the paper with the words or representation of their stressful situation. Let the power of the chant rise as all the members place their paper into the fire. Continue to chant until the power reaches its peak and then each member may again toss a small handful herbs into the cauldron and breath in the relaxation. Keep the conversation light if you choose to just hang out after the spell. Bask in the full moon light and rest under the power of the Mead Moon.

Chapter Ten
August - Corn Moon & Lughnasadh

August brings us to the eighth month of our modern calendar and the celebrations of the first harvest at Lughnasadh and the Corn Moon. This is a time of harvesting the gifts we have nurtured through the year, making the first fresh breads, collecting herbs for storage and making offerings to the Earth. Lughnasadh is the Celtic festival of the first harvest, dedicated to Lugh, the Celtic Lord of the Sun and Craftsmanship, among other things. For the Otherkin that is following the lunar cycle, this is a month full of opportunities for ritual work and honoring the cycles of the Earth and Moon.

Through the lunar cycle, the Corn Moon is the time that we will see the first fruits of our labors of the year. If we have planned carefully, this should be a time of great joy as our projects move to a fruitful time, whether they are agricultural or not. What first began as a thought in January, is now bearing the fruits and seeds of life and your work will continue if you have reached this far. Just remember to continue to plant those seeds in the future and create perennial growth, as well as short-term projects in your life. The first harvest is not time to say we are done with this project, as first or early harvests may not bear much fruit. But remember that there is a possibility for three more opportunities to harvest in the months to come.

Among Otherkin covens, this time of year is for honoring the Earth for its bounty and recognizing the growing shadows, as nights get longer. In pagan circles, this was the time of year for honoring the many sun gods such as Lugh, in their decline. Whether our Otherkin aspects are related to the day or night, the time of the first harvest has much to offer us, just as we make offerings to the spirits and the Earth. Covens may wish to gather herbs from their gardens, as well as from the wild or share in homemade bread as you can. Shapeshifting rites can also be performed to aid us in understanding this time of year and letting our wild selves out to roam near fields and forests in the twilight.

At the festival of the first harvest on August 1st, Lughnasadh is a time for the Otherkin to recognize the blessings of their efforts up to this time of year. Far too often, modern people place an expectancy upon what our "harvests," in life should be. From our paycheck at the end of the week, to how much we should receive for payment in the sale of a home or handmade goods, we expect to make enough to do whatever we need. This is not the way nature based life works. The old sayings, *"count your blessings,"* as well as "don't count your *chickens before they hatch,"* applies much in the way our ancestors lived and believed in the harvests of life. Modern society takes away the virtue of patience in our endeavors and replaces it with instant gratification. This point of view can keep us from seeing our true blessings as they unfold in the time that is right for us and whatever project we are currently working on. Before the ritual of Lughnasadh, spend some time really considering the good that has come about in your life in this time of year and from your recent endeavors, whether a return to college has been made or a business and/or new career or relationship are being started. The first year in anything new is often the most difficult, but if we can stay the path, we will see the fruits of our labors multiply over time.

Otherkin Lughnasadh Ritual

After the coven has spent some time in the days prior to the rite contemplating the blessings received, sacrifices made or lessons learned, then gather the needed items for the ritual and begin. For this rite, you may wish to gather at the edge of the forest, in or near a field, or near a lake or stream, as would be customary for this time of year. Build a fire pit or small campfire prior to the working and be careful of any dry plants or trees near your ritual space.

Need: Sheaves of wheat and/or corn dollies
(any harvest representations such as the cornucopia, ears of corn, bread, grains, etc)
Fire pit or campfire
Mugwort & wormwood
Smudge bowl
Feather Fan
Drum & beater
Rattles
Ritual Axe
Medicine Shield
Journals & pens

Set up the altar area with the coven Medicine Shield in the northern most point of the circle. The smudge bowl, feather fan, drum and rattles, and ritual axe can be placed here too. The fire pit or campfire can be made in the center of the circle, so long as you don't get the fire too big. Harvest representations should be held by members of the coven until time to make offerings during the rite. After the ritual area is set up, the priest/ess or shaman stands before them to speak…

> *"Upon this evening, we gather to honor the Earth in this season of the first harvest. The rites of Lughnasadh bring us the first fruits of our labors in life, whether from the grains harvested in the fields, herbs grown in our gardens, or new ways of life created upon our path. This is a time of offering something back to our Earth Mother, to ask for her assistance in bringing forth the kind of life that we seek, the kind of life that is right in our hearts for us to walk in this earthly path. Spirits of the Earth, Spirits of the Harvest, wild spirits of forest and field, come forth and accept our offerings upon this eve, grant us your blessing in this rite."*

The priest/ess or shaman motions for all to begin placing their offerings under the medicine shield at the north of the ritual area. Each member moves up to place their offerings and makes a short moment from their heart about the blessings they seek in this rite, and in their life.

Then the next member moves up to the medicine shield to do the same. After the offerings are placed under the coven medicine shield, the priest/ess or shaman of the coven raises the ritual axe and speaks again…

> *"By the axe, we seek our harvest in this rite. It is by the axe, that we transform our spirits and our lives. By the axe so do we harvest from the Earth and fields. By the axe, we create and by the axe, we destroy. By the axe, we journey tonight, to find the wisdom of the spirits in the Otherworld, to guide us in our path in this life."*

The drumming begins, as the priest/ess or shaman lifts up the smudge bowl, filled with mugwort and wormwood. The herbs are ignited from the campfire and the smoke wafted over each member with the feather fan to aid their journeying abilities. The priest/ess or shaman picks up the rattle and gently cleanses each member before returning to the northern point of the circle. The shaman or priest/ess now take a seat near the medicine shield, and the drums pick up the pace. The journey begins as all in the coven slip into the in-between worlds. The journey at this time of year should be for us to find guidance in our projects and life challenges. Going to speak to those spirits and asking for the guidance and blessing can be the difference between success and failure in whatever projects are working on.

After a time of journeying, the drum sounds to call all participants back. When everyone has returned from their journey, all coven members should give their thanks to the spirits and place the offerings slowly into the fire then the priest/ess or shaman may close the circle. You can now spend some time talking around the campfire about what each member saw or experienced in the Otherworld. Pay close attention to signals received in these journeys and write them down so that they will make sense at a later time.

Corn Moon Ritual

For the ritual of the Corn Moon, try to gather in a field or large clearing in the forest, to have space for the rite to really flow with energy. Understand that participants may need to take turns between drumming or playing flutes and dancing, unless they are skilled at both. It can be difficult to play an instrument while bouncing about but this can aid the energy further. Clothing can be optional but be respectful. Gather the needed items and begin.

Need: Pan flutes (Or other instruments if available)
    Drums
    Rattles
    Campfire
    Stones or flour for circle
    Stoneware bowl
    Mugwort and Wormwood
    Feather Fan
    Medicine Shield
    Staff or wand
    Harvest offerings

A large circle of stones or flour is cast on the ground. The campfire is made outside the circle, but nearby. The Medicine Shield is placed at the northern most point of the circle with the feather fan, stoneware bowl of herbs, and staff close by. Musical instruments may be inside or outside of the circle according to the participants desire to be in the circle for the deeper aspects of the rite. Those in the circle are invoking and evoking the spirits that they work with, to bring on a state of mild to moderate possession. Under the influence of these spirits, they can learn new things about life, spirits and magic, etc. By calling on Otherkin harvest spirits and totems, we will align ourselves with greater energy and wisdom to accomplish our goals in life, love and joy. This is similar to the shapeshifting rite, where all who will be shifting, remain within the circle. All who wish to become temporarily possessed should remain within the circle.

The priest/ess or shaman of the coven moves to the northern point of the circle and lifts his or her staff. All members that wish to participate in the rite from within the circle should enter now or remain outside of the circle. The priest/ess or shaman raises the staff in silence for a moment and channels their energy into the chant:

> *"I cast thee sacred circle of power*
> *Focused here from this hour!"*

The chant continues as the priest/ess walks the circle three times clock-wise, empowering it with energy from the staff. After the circle is cast, they return to the northern point and speak...

"We gather this night of the Corn Moon to call upon the Spirits of the Harvest and Lunar Magick. We call to the satyrs and nymphs, wights and elves, forest daemons and wild spirits! Hail thee! Come forth in this night, and join us in our revelry, under the music and rhythms that you gave to mankind, so long ago. The ways of the wild spirits are here and alive in this night of the harvest season! Let those who stand within the circle be fortunate enough to be granted your wisdom, as you walk within their flesh for a brief period tonight."

The priest/ess or shaman lifts the smudge bowl and ignites the herbs of mugwort and wormwood, to open the psychic channels and let the person work in the darkness while keeping some protection. The shaman or priest/ess wafts the smoke, in billows over the participants within the circle. As each moves through the smoke of the incense, they receive the blessing of the priest/ess or shaman of the group, to further guard them within the rite. After the smudging and blessing is complete, the music begins. A flute is heard, gently in the breeze, as a drumbeat softly joins in. The shaman or priest/ess raises a rattle and begins chanting, or singing a *"Song of No Words,"* as is common to shamanic traditions. It is by this signal that the flutes and drumming rise in volume and power. Dancers are free to follow the rhythms of the music, made by those tranced into instruments. Each member within the circle is free to invoke or evoke any spirit or totem that they are connected to. The purpose of the circle here is to create a place for this energy to take hold, for possession to happen in a safe environment. The more often a place is used for rituals, the more easily these rites will be effective.

The music and dancing can continue for a while, as each member is able to revel in the rhythm and flow of the drums and flutes. If the members are able to achieve the trance state needed to receive a mild possession, whether by totem animals or other spirits, then keep a watch on that individual and find out a name to any spirits claiming to be in possession of someone. After the dancing and music begin to slow, the priest/ess or shaman stand again at the northern point of the circle, in front of the medicine shield.

> *"Spirits of the Harvest! Spirits of the Moon! We give our thanks to thee, for all your wild blessings and joy on this night of the Corn Moon! Accept these offerings in our sincerest gratitude. We thank you for this time of revelry and joy. Let us be fruitful in our path in life and follow the ways of the spirits. We give our thanks to thee! Hail and Blessed Be!"*

The coven slowly brings offerings to the campfire and the shaman or priest/ess of the coven closes the circle, by walking widdershins with the staff around it chanting:

> *"I return this energy into space*
> *Thank you for this time of grace!"*

The coven may spend time resting and talking about the experiences of the ritual. Be sure to write down any information received from the ritual to contemplate for later.

Chapter Eleven
September – Harvest Moon
& Autumn Equinox

The month of September brings us to the Harvest Moon and the Autumn Equinox. This is the second harvest of the year, both agriculturally and according to our projects and path. While the Harvest Moon invites us to drink in the divine in balance and celebrate our growth as we reap the benefits of our work, the Autumn Equinox celebrates the beginning of the darker aspects of the path and year. This is the opposite time of spring and growing into longer nights than days. The autumn season should be special to all Otherkin as it represents the energy of death and change throughout the course of our life. The fall is a sacred time for the shapeshifter and a special time for gathering among the coven.

Otherkin coven rituals for the Harvest Moon should be centered on Shapeshifting Rites, astral sabbat workings and any work that utilizes the darker aspects of the path. Vampirism and lycanthropic rituals can be created and used amongst the coven, as well as brews and incense for reaching into the darkness. This time of year makes invoking the harvest spirits and darker totems within us such as the crow or owl, easier and we may be able to take flight on great wings at twilight. Developing a mastery over the mind in astral travel is highly suggested for this type of ritual working or journey.

The Autumn Equinox celebrates the turn of the year from light back into darkness. For those following the moon through the year, this should bring your projects to a more fruitful and bountiful time period. The autumn equinox is often called Mabon in pagan circles and is a time of witchcraft and magic, as herbs and plants are harvested with much celebration among the coven. As mentioned previously, Mabon is a time to work with darker totems such as the wolf, owl, crow, fox and cat spirits and these may be worked with by Otherkin shapeshifters during this time of year for the greatest benefit. Many early pagan deities and spirits played a big part in the harvest season and should be revered among the Otherkin at this time of year, as well.

The autumn season has many spirits attached to it from different traditions all over the world. This time of year combines the harvest energy of rewards and bounty with the current of death and change, as the crops are harvested or animals are slaughtered for food through the winter. The following is a list of spirits and daemons that can be contacted during this time of year and may be helpful to understanding your harvests in life and how to create a bountiful harvest in the years to come. These spirits also aid us in understanding the necessity of the current of death and change in the world.

Spirits & Daemons of
Autumn Harvests & the Current of Death

Baalberith – daemon Prince of Dying, Lord of Pacts & Covenants, protection of the dead, death and rebirth, may be as a scribe for demonic work

Babael – daemon keeper of graves, gentler than Euronymous for rituals of death and rebirth and protection of cemeteries

Beelzebuth – daemon of money, prosperity, & luck

Dionysus – wild pagan spirit of the Hunt, grapes & wine, shamanic ecstasy and intoxication, sexual healing, leader of the satyrs

Euronymous – daemon of death, rebirth, new beginnings, and the celebration of All Hallows

Frey & Freya – Norse god and goddess of magic, fertility and the harvest, shapeshifting, and the Hunt

Green Man – may be Dionysus, Odin, Pan or many other spirits, the Green man of the harvest has been worshipped for millennia.

Leviathan – daemon serpent of the west and the water element, autumn equinox, initiation, emotions,

Mephistopheles – famous in the Faustian tradition Mephisto is the daemon keeper of the book of death, Pacts, sorcery, knowledge, and secrets.

Norns – Norse sisters of Wyrd, Urd rules the past, Verdandi the present, and Skuld the youth who scores the future. I took the liberty of adding them here as they are ancient spirits of the runes and practicing divination may be important during your harvest season.

Nymphs – wild spirits of forests and lakes, rivers and mountains, can be called upon for learning music, magic, protection of mothers and children and of course aid in the harvests of the year.

Pan – wild half man- half goat spirit from ancient Greece. Goat men exist in stories from around the world; they are fertility spirits of the harvest in forest, flock and field.

Satyrs – wild goat men such as Pan or Dionysus, spirits of male fertility, music and harvests.

Verrier – daemoness of herbal knowledge and healing

Verrine – daemoness of healing

This will conclude this list of spirits of the autumn season and the current of death and change. This gives you over fourteen spirits to start off your harvest season and learn the ways of alignment with nature and the cycles of the moon. These spirits can be invoked and worked with through the autumn season to help in teaching us the deeper ways of nature and change. I have worked with most of these spirits over the course of years and have had great success with them. You may wish to journey or research for sigils or tools for invocation before working on your needs. Invoke them in your circles and magic to teach you the ways of harvest in life and love.

Harvest Moon Ritual

Even a man who is pure in heart,
And says his prayers by night
May become a wolf when the wolf's bane blooms
And the autumn moon is bright!

From the original motion picture
"The Wolf Man" 1941

The Harvest Moon is inextricably tied to images of traditional witchcraft from early American settlers. I feel the above poem from almost seventy-five years ago reflects early beliefs in the supernatural and may be as a good basis for the Otherkin Shapeshifter, Initiate or Devotee. This Rite of the Harvest Moon is intended to reflect the ancient ways and traditions as a part of Otherkin ceremony and devotion. This is an initiation and devotional rite of death and rebirth as we harvest a new understanding of our life on Earth. Initiates and long-term practitioners alike can benefit from this ritual, as we devote ourselves to the path of the powers of the Moon and claim our inner power to shapeshift in spirit and change our life. Covens may incorporate any pagan celebrations for the harvest itself during or after this ritual gathering. Feasting on breads and fruits from the years harvest are traditional Wiccan/pagan fare. If gathering outdoors, the circle may be illuminated with torches, allowing for space within the circle for shapeshifting rites. Gather the needed items under the full moon and begin.

Need: 2 Silver or white candles
    Flour or stones for circle
    Harvest offerings
    Staff or wand

Use flour or stones to create a large circle for the ritual. Place the silver or white candles to the eastern corner of the circle with the offerings between the candles. Initiates or devotees may be nude, robed, or as scantily clad as weather permits. If you have very many members of the coven that are devoting themselves or being initiated, you may let them stand around the inner portion of the circle. When you are ready, the priest/ess or shaman of the group stands near the east corner and speaks...

"We gather this night of the Harvest Moon, to initiate and devote our selves in body, mind and spirit, to the path of the powers of the Moon. We make an offering to the spirits and daemons of the moon, that they may hear us and grant us new powers, of shapeshifting, powers of wisdom and insight, powers of magic, upon this harvest night."

The priest/ess or shaman lifts the staff (or wand) and pointing it at the circle of stones or flour begins to cast the circle, chanting.

*"I cast thee, sacred circle of power
Be focused here, from this hour!"*

The priest/ess walks the circle three times around then, finishes at the eastern corner. He or she ignites the candles, looks to the rising moon and speaks...

> *"Spirits and daemons of the Moon, we call upon thee in this night, as we devote our selves to the ways of the moon, the ways of the spirits. We walk this sacred path of power, to attune with the ways of nature. We seek within our minds, our hearts, and our spirits for wisdom and guidance. We call to you as individuals, and as one!"*

A chant begins among the coven members within the circle. This can be created as a chant of devotion to the path of the Moon and the Earth, or devotion to your spirit guide, be they daemon, pagan, or Other. Creating a chant for the coven and incorporating your own ideals and beliefs in the season, shapeshifting, etc, will be a way to empower the coven and give a longer lasting devotion to the path.

> *"I walk the path of the sacred Moon*
> *Upon the night I fly*
> *By the spirits' twists and tunes*
> *I'm a wolf within the rye!"*

The chant builds among the coven to raise energy for the group. Each member may begin to use their own methods of shapeshifting within the circle, chanting, dancing and allowing the energy of the Harvest Moon and ritual to overwhelm them. Allow the shapeshifting work to go on for a time then, when the coven members grow tired, the priest/ess or shaman of the coven may close the circle. Feasting may begin at this time and leave the offerings somewhere near the ritual space, under a tree etc. Be sure to clean up the area before leaving.

Autumn Equinox Ritual

For the ritual of the Autumn Equinox, gather in or near a field, or at the edge of a forest or lake before sunset. This rite is intended to aid the practitioner in attaining new abilities or working with different totems in journey and in life. I know that it is not always possible to pick which totems will guide us in journeys, but with a little effort, spells or rites, it can be done. Totems of the harvest mentioned earlier in this chapter are highly suggested and each member of the Otherkin coven may wish to bring a fetish item of their chosen totem for the ritual. Gather the needed items and you may begin.

Need: Drum & beater
    Rattle
    Smudge wand (cedar or sage)
    Fetish item (from each member)
    Smudge bowl
    Incense of mugwort & wormwood
    Fire pit or campfire
    Feather fan (if available)
    Medicine shield
    Blankets for warmth and seating (as needed)
    Journals & pens

Use the fire pit or build a campfire in the center of the gathering area. Place the coven Medicine Shield at the northern most corner of the circle or hang in a nearby tree. The ritual should begin with the shaman or priest/ess of the coven igniting a cedar or sage smudge wand and performing a cleansing, first on him or her self then, on each member of the coven. This is to clear away any negative energy to allow the energy of the ritual to flow through each participant. Cleansing may also be performed upon fetish items if deemed necessary. Following the cleansing, an incense of mugwort and wormwood may be ignited in the smudge bowl. Waft the smoke over each coven member with the feather fan to empower his or her psychic abilities and allow the practitioner to work in the darkness while being protected. Once the smudging is complete, the shaman or priest/ess may shake the rattle over each member to further cleanse and empower the aura. All members may take their places and let the drumming begin gently as the shaman speaks...

> *"Upon this evening of the Autumn Equinox, we gather here to journey to the spirit worlds. We give our thanks and send our invitations to any spirit totem or daemon, which would choose to aid us in this journey. By this rite of the harvest season, we fly forth, upon dark wings, and in silent and swift runnings, to attain new wisdom and guidance. Let us each attain contact with the totem or spirit that we seek; to fly upon black wings in the evening*

sun. To move in stealth and silence as the fox or wolf, to screech and call through the darkness as the owl spirit. We journey between the worlds for wisdom and new abilities. Spirits be with us!

Each coven member takes a place, either seated or lying down near the fire pit. They hold their fetishes close as the drumming begins to pick up the pace and an intense rhythm signifies the beginning of the journey. Coven members should try to visualize being together in the place that you are physically located to begin the journey. This is a middle world journey and should mostly take place in the spirit realm next to this world. The things you see and hear should be remembered to the best of your ability. Let your spirit soar upon the drumbeat, through the forest, above the field, to see the coven members lying still upon the earth, gathered around the fire. Let the journey take you where it will, listen to your guides during this journey and learn as much as you can. When you are ready, or when the journey drummer begins to call you back, make a final listen to your spirit guides, and give them thanks for any information you have received then slowly return to normal consciousness.

When everyone has returned from the journey and gotten their bearings back on this realm of being, take a moment of silent reverence for the spirits that have guided you and for the experiences you have just witnessed. After the moment of silence, the shaman or priest/ess of the coven stands to speak...

"Upon this evening we have experienced many wondrous things and traveled to many wonderful places in the spirit realm. We give our thanks for the bounty of the harvest in this night and for the guidance we have received. We thank thee spirits, one and all!! Hail thee!!"

The coven calls "Hail thee!"

After the rite has ended, you may share stories and experiences of your journeys and ask for insight about things that may not be clear from the shaman or priest/ess of the coven. This will give you time to reflect on your journey into the middle realm and allow each of you to gain an understanding of your spiritual experience from a broader perspective. Be sure to record you experiences in your journal and share your stories afterward. If you wish you may gather and feast, or leave offerings to the spirits before cleaning up.

Chapter Twelve
October – Blood Moon & Samhain

October bring us to the tenth month and a very dramatic and dark part of the yearly cycle. As days grow cooler in the fall, the Blood Moon brings forth the time of death and the current of change. The Celtic pagan festival of Samhain, pronounced *"sow – een,"* is the last harvest of the year and a time for slaughtering the livestock and hunting to store meat during the winter months. Late autumn harvests have always been very important for those following the cycles of the moon and nature, as this was all the food left for the year, picked and stored away for winter. October also brings to mind the season of the dead, and is a time of honoring the ancestors while the veil between worlds is thin, and lighting candles to light the way for the dead that wander the earth. For those who follow the moon in this year, the last harvest at Samhain brings you close to the completion of your yearly projects. If this is a perennial growing project, you will have much to look forward to in the future, so long as you nourish your growth and change, encouraging root growth through the winter months. The Blood Moon for the Otherkin is a special time of traditional witchcraft in imagery and darker magical works such as necromancy and the vampiric arts.

Otherkin rites of the Blood Moon should be centered around the current of death, rebirth and transformation.

The spiritual realization and understanding that change is the only constant in life can be attained through meditation and contemplation in this month of gloom and death. Vampiric magick can be worked in a coven setting with more than just drinking blood or energy. This may be for practice at attaining vampiric extremities to drain the life force or using the shadows in astral and dream workings. The Blood Moon is also the time in which the daemons of death are closest and the devil walks with earthly feet. In this, the crossroads may be called upon for many different purposes in ritual and spellcraft. Crossroads are not often mentioned in modern witchcraft, although there are both pagan deities and Hoodoo spirits that work at the crossroads of life. Both sets of pagan and Hoodoo spirits are connected to the crossroads and the cemetery i.e., realms of the dead.

The following is a list of six spirits that are best contacted from the crossroads or cemeteries although other methods and places can be used. Keep in mind that spirits of the crossroads are trickster spirits that can aid in removing the blocks on your path and many other things. While many of these spirits are connected with All Hallows Eve, crossroads workings can be performed at any time of year deemed necessary. In my opinion and experience, they are highly evolved in their spiritual understanding of life, love and freedom. They can take you to places and give understanding that may not be possible without them. I realize that there are many spirits listed in this book, so for these purposes I have chosen to keep this listing short. See the beginning of the

Autumn Equinox in chapter eleven for more information on daemons and spirits of death and change.

6 Spirits of the Crossroads

Exu – Afro-Brazilian trickster spirit, master of roads, protection, healer, may be tied to many different spirits from the African Diaspora and Hoodoo traditions

Hecate – Lunar Goddess of Witchcraft, shapeshifting, Queen of the Crossroads, magic, protection, fertility, vengeance, wisdom, justice, birth, death, necromancy keeper of the keys of life.

Papa Legba – spirit of New Orleans Voodoo, trickster spirit of the crossroads, remover of blockages on the path, he can grant a great number of things to the practitioner if approached properly. May be as Exu, Eshu Ellegua, and many others.

The "Devil" – this is a highly controversial topic, even among witches. The *"Devil"* may be seen by the Otherkin as many different spirits, from many traditions. At any rate, the devil is the black man of the witch's sabbat and a granter of many things. Calling upon him does not *"Damn your soul,"* but may offer a new found freedom by calling the powers of the forest and darkness itself. This may also be used as a generic term for the satyrs, Pan, Dionysus, Exu, Legba, and a host of others that Christianity "demonized."

Tuveries – daemon from the grimoire tradition, teaches the secrets of trivium (crossroads) particularly a three-way crossroads, reveals hidden treasure, and can assist in travel over bodies of water

Zagam – daemon mentioned in many grimoires, dark spirit of the crossroads and necromancy

Ritual of the Crossroads

Many different rituals and spells can be performed at a crossroads. Some meditation on the subject of the crossroads in general, can reveal much in the way of understanding what it is for and how it helps. Crossroads are places of making decisions, and changing directions, within us and in life. This is a place of criss-crossing energies, and at one time in our history were places to meet others, traders, merchants, etc., which may or may not have been good. Many things such as remnants from spells can be destroyed at a crossroads or you can give yourself over to the spirits found here for new abilities, love interests, etc. Crossroads offer us choices, and the road we take in those choices will determine our future circumstances. The magic of the Crossroads guides us in divination in this aspect and can grant us an understanding of our life from another perspective. In many folk tales, the crossroads is a place of learning, especially music and talent with an instrument, which means that crossroads spirits are teachers in some sense and of some subjects. There is very powerful magic to be worked at the crossroads late in the night.

Rituals of the Crossroads are often performed at midnight or in the wee hours of morning, just before sunrise. You may align crossroads rituals with the full or new moons, holidays, sabbats, etc. as may be dictated by your needs or the time of the occurrence. A crossroads ritual may be difficult to work as a coven due to the location and the amount people but if you can find a remote location it may be a great success for all involved. If you choose to go to the crossroads for magical reasons, try this simple working.

Choose a magical tool that you own such as a wand, staff, musical instrument, crystal, etc. Take a small offering such as tobacco or rum, to the crossroads for the spirits in exchange. Sometimes they may not accept the offering but will let you know what they want in return. Make your choices carefully! Give yourself enough time to get to the crossroads at just before midnight or if you chose, just before dawn. Call upon one of the Crossroads spirits listed above or one that you have a connection with, from your own *"tradition,"* and ask them to aid you in learning how to use and work with this item better, perhaps even the crossroads itself. Open your arms to the sky with this item in your receptive hand and call the spirits of the crossroads aloud.

> *"Spirits of the Crossroads! Exu! Papa Legba! Hecate! Zagam! Hear my call unto you! I ask you in this night to grant me the abilities I seek, to work with this magical instrument! Teach me the ways, in days to come of greater powers with this tool! Hail thee spirits of the Crossroads!"*

Stay at the crossroads and think about what you would like to be able to do with this magical tool or musical instrument. Be sure you remain at the crossroads until after midnight/ sunrise and place your offering close by. Leave in a different direction than the one you came from and do not leave for any reason before the spell is complete (before midnight or sunrise) as you may miss your chance for abilities or whatever else you asked for. Keep a watchful eye out for any spirits that may run by in the night or early morning.

According to folktales from the American south, *"the devil will run by you at some point, or he may stop and ask you for the instrument. He will tune it or show you how to use it then, give it back to you. After this has happened, you can return home a different direction than you came from and you will be able to perform greater feats with your newly attained abilities."*

Blood Moon Ritual (#1)

As the Blood Moon is a time of hunting and sacrifice in preparation for the winter, so this is a shamanic rite of hunting. A rite such as this can be used for many different things, all-depending upon what is being hunted. Do we seek or hunt for greater wisdom? Financial gains? New abilities? Or do we truly hunt for revenge, intending to cause pain and devastation to someone? This is for you to decide. The shamanic rites of hunting date back millennia over a wide range of cultures. The shaman of the tribe used his shamanic journeying ability to aid in the hunt from a spiritual perspective for his or her people. The shaman's success or failure in the spiritual hunt was considered reflective of the physical hunt amongst the tribesmen and warriors. So, this too, may be considered before taking upon yourself or your coven, the rite of shamanic hunting.

The main tool used in shamanic hunting is a short spear or *"shaman's arrow."* This tool is used to remove blockages and obtrusive energy in the spirit body for healing, or to kill an enemy that has wronged you. Each shamanic practitioner should make his or her own arrow for this purpose and you may need to make one for healing and a separate one for *"soul-hunting"* and darker magic as your needs dictate. A good sturdy, straight branch of willow, about the length of your arm can be used for healing or dark magic. If you can make your own arrowheads, this is even better, but you can also purchase them from a variety of stores and flea markets. Smooth the willow switch with sandpaper and attach your arrowhead to the willow shaft by cutting a notch into the end and then using hemp thread or leather cording to tie it together. I will make the suggestion of coloring the arrow shaft during the creation rite, so as to aid in capturing the energy accordingly. If your arrow is for healing and extraction purposes, you may wish to color it white, green, blue, purple, or even red, representing the life force of the blood. If it is intended for harm, color it black with some charcoal or lampblack (soot from the smoke of an oil lantern or high burning candle). If you wish to use various colors for different purposes, being more specific than I am here, then so be it. The important thing is to not confuse a healing arrow with a destructive one or to cleanse it thoroughly between uses. When you have finished crafting your shaman's arrow you will need to empower it with a creation rite of your own design. Give it energy and intention for its use and then either keep it on or near your altar or cover it and put it away for safe keeping until it is needed.

This rite may be performed as a solitary practitioner or as a coven with a little ingenuity. If many among the coven can journey then each can use the drumbeat to go into the Otherworld with their own arrows to hunt for themselves. I am going to use the term *"target,"* here to mean whatever it is that you are hunting or pursuing. As I said previously, this is up to you. If you can, perform this rite outdoors in a forest or field, or near a lake or river. Gather the needed items and begin.

> Need: Drum & beater
>> Rattle
>> Shaman's Arrow
>> Fire pit or campfire
>> Blankets to sit or lie on
>> Smudge wand (cedar or sage)
>> Smudge Bowl
>> Incense of mugwort and wormwood
>> (incense may be crafted as needs dictate)
>> Medicine Shield
>> Journals & pens

For this rite, create a campfire or place the fire pit in the center of your gathering area. You may place the Medicine Shield to the north for coven gatherings, but if you wish, you can place the Medicine Shield in the direction that most suits your needs. This may be the east, south, west, north, center, or anything in between. Each direction has a meaning and purpose and each can aid in your magic for spiritual hunting. Weather permitting, you may also use torches to light the area after dark. The priest/ess or shaman of the coven will smudge him or her self, then all members of the coven to cleanse away unnecessary energy. Next the priest/ess or shaman will shake the rattle around each member to remove excess energy before beginning. Now, the shaman ignites the incense smudge and wafts the smoke over each coven member for empowerment before the ritual fully begins. Remember that mugwort and wormwood allow the practitioner to open the psychic channels and reach into the darkness while still keeping some protection around them. When all members of the coven have been cleansed and empowered, the priest/ess or shaman of the coven speaks...

"Upon this night of the Blood Moon, we gather here to journey between the worlds and hunt within the spirit realms. By the ways of the Moon, we take up the sacred arrow, which gives us the power to heal or harm. By the ways of the Shapeshifters, under the moonlit night, we fly between the realms in our Wild Hunt! Mother

Moon! Grant us your Blessing in this rite, as we seek and hunt through the forests of the spirit realm, and in the physical world!"

A gentle drumbeat begins and coven members take their places on the blankets and holding their arrows as the shaman speaks again...

"Let us attain victory as we Hunt our targets in this night!"

The drumbeat jumps in pace and intensity as the shaman begins a chant, a song of No Words, to encourage the journeying among the coven. Each member of the coven should visualize themselves being where they are in the physical realm. Again, this gives us connections in the spirit world with the rest of the coven. You may find yourself with your power animal or spirit guide, taking you through the forest, to hunt your target. The thrill of the hunt in the spirit world feels exhilarating as you suddenly find the target you set out for, lurking deep in the forest. Now the question is only, can you defeat this target and gain victory? The target begins to speak to you, mocking you to come forward. Your power animal pushes you to attack, so feeling the arrow in your hand, you rush forward and stab at the target with the arrow point. The arrowhead slashes past the targets face, a deep red gash, slowly emerging on its cheek. Now you rush again, knowing it is stunned, and this is your chance to attain victory. The target, tries to move away, but this time your arrow pierces his side, blood flows freely, and your target stares up as he falls to the ground. You hear the drumbeat calling you back, and you give thanks to your guide for their help as you pull the arrow from the targets side. You make a short prayer to give thanks for your victory, and the loss of your targets life. Then you fly back to the clearing where you see the rest of the coven moving about. You hold the arrow in your hand, and thank your power animal one last time, as he gives you a bit of advice about your endeavors of this ritual. You understand, and nodding your head at him, you open your eyes. Your target is dead, you have attained victory. Allow yourself time to awaken and write your results in your journal.

After everyone has recorded their results, the priest/ ess or shaman of the coven may speak again of the events of the evening. The coven is encouraged to share the stories and experiences of the journey of hunting on the Blood Moon. Give thanks to the spirits and relax in your victory.

Author's Note If you take upon yourself the journey of hunting and are meeting an adversary, be careful. If you fail in this journey, and your target wins, this can manifest as sickness or pains, in some way in your body. What happens in the mind and spirit realm will be reflected in the physical one. You have been warned!!

Rite of the Blood Moon (#2)

Because much dark magic can be worked in the month of October, under the Blood Moon and Samhain, I am adding a second ritual for choices and ideas among the Otherkin covens. This is a ritual for those of a vampiric or darker persuasion among the coven of Otherkin. Keep in mind that vampiric practices are much more than just draining energy from a victim and I believe that one can use some vampiric abilities and not necessarily have to claim vampirism as your only *"other self."* It is simply a matter of understanding that all things have a dark side that can be scary or freakish at times. We also go through various changes, transformations and evolution on our path to spiritual fulfillment. Darkness does not have to be the whole of the path, but it is always part of the path, depending upon our choices of focus and attention.

This is a rite of using trance to attain your astral shadow in the physical world. While this can be used for vampiric practices, draining energy from someone, it can also be used for moving about undetected or only subtly noticed as a spirit. In this way, the shamanic Otherkin transcends the flesh and moves through the realms of the dead. I will state that if one among you is more adept at vampiric practices, draining energy, etc, you may wish to focus the coven's energy on that one person. This will allow him or her to be able to focus this energy into forming a shadow in the astral to move about with. Just be sure that they won't turn against you once they attain this ability. Power such as this can be corrupting if not used wisely.

A quick note before we begin. I realize that this is similar to a Middle world journey, being based in the earthly plane, but the difference is in the creation of a shadow form to move about with. This is also the reasoning for the earlier middle world journeys and seeing the place that you are currently located. This is advanced astral projection using shamanic journey to attain a new ability. This could be called, *"vampiric shamanism,"* for lack of a better term. This ritual has been created from my own early workings in vampire meditations and using the astral shadow.

For this rite of the Blood Moon you will need a large room or chamber that can be darkened, with the only illumination being candlelight. You will also need space for the coven to gather around a large inverted pentagram drawn upon the floor. If you have a large banner or flag with the inverted pentagram on it you may use it here. For the coven working, let all who will participate, lie around the circle of the pentagram. Or as suggested earlier, place the vampiric practitioner on the pentagram and let the coven be seated around them. Coven members may or may not "see" the shadow form over himself or herself or the vampire of the coven, but with time and practice, it will first be felt, then physically seen moving about. This can be scary especially at first; so don't panic when it happens. This is true advancement in dark magic.

Need: Five Black pillar candles
Inverted Pentagram (drawn in flour, chalk, or use a banner)
Incense of wormwood
Smudge Bowl
Drum & beater

Draw the pentagram upon the floor inverted so that the single point is directed to the south or west. Place a large black pillar candle at each point, being sure to leave room if a single vampire is to lie upon the pentagram. The smudge bowl with incense of wormwood should be placed between the top two points. If all coven members will be lying around the circle, be sure that the room is a comfortable temperature to encourage the working's success. You may be nude if you wish, or lightly robed for the ritual.

When all is in place, the priest/ess or shaman of the coven will ignite the incense in the smudge bowl and begin to waft the smoke about the room, and speak...

"With this dark and sacred smoke, we call upon the powers of the Blood Moon! Grant us the focus to rise as a shadow, formed in the night, to move beyond the realm of the flesh and into the realms of the dead! We invoke thee, Onoskelis, daemoness and succubus of the darken realms. Spider daemon of the blue flame! Grant us the power! We invoke thee!

The coven chants: "We invoke thee, Onoskelis!"

The priest/ess or shaman of the group places the smudge bowl back between the top two points of the pentagram while the coven still chants. A drumbeat begins as the shaman ignites the candles, beginning with the single point at the bottom and working around the circle. The chant of the coven fades as the priest/ess or shaman speaks again...

"Upon this night, we form the astral shadow! With the aid of daemoness, Onoskelis, we rise between the worlds of the living and the dead! Onoskelis! Onoskelis! Onoskelis! ..."

The coven continues to chant the daemoness' name as the drumbeat rises in tempo. When the drumbeat reaches the shamanic trancing beat, the chant fades as each member of the coven lies back, or holds out their hands to project energy into the single vampire in the circle. If each member lies back, they must intensely visualize themselves from above their bodies and begin to *"see"* the astral shadow forming over them. This is your form for this projection. If your consciousness is not attached to the form, you may leave excess negative energy floating about the room after the rite is over. Move your consciousness into this black mass or cloud and see from within this form, into the room or home around you. If the coven is focused on one member, this black cloud should be visualized as hovering and forming above the single practitioner lying in the center of the pentagram. When you have the shadow form around you, begin to move from within it, circling about the ceiling or moving into another room. This is the reason for not casting a circle, as it can trap you in one place if it is effective. Move about the home, or move out into the night sky and look about with the cloud of shadow energy around you. Experience this for as long as you can, then when you hear the drumbeat calling you back, float back into the room, and hover over your body. Let the visualization of the cloud fade away the blackness so that you are you again. See in your visualization this cloud dissipating and fading from view. This too, is important so that the energy does not cause problems for the home's inhabitants. After the shadow dissipates, settle back into your body and open your eyes.

The coven may share in their experiences with this ritual and write results in your journal. The priest/ess or shaman and the whole coven should give thanks to Onoskelis, aloud before extinguishing the candles. You may wish to burn a smudge of cedar or sage and open windows for a few minutes to clear away any negative energy remaining in the room, unless you plan on practicing it again in the same place at a later time.

Samhain Ritual

Samhain, or as we know it, Halloween, has long been a time of honoring the ancestors and those who have passed away during the year. This rite for the

Otherkin coven follows the old traditions of lighting candles to light the way for the dead and honoring the ancestors from long ago. If you wish, daemons or spirits of death and the dead may be honored as your coven or individual beliefs dictate. I have in the recent past tried to blend the Hoodoo practice of leaving a small amount of money (coins) near a cemetery gate in exchange for graveyard soil, but found that Babael does not want it. I found the exact amount of change that I left at the cemetery on my front sidewalk upon returning home. Coincidence? I don't know, but I haven't done it since. Different areas and cities will also have different laws about cemetery admittance after dark so be careful and don't get arrested for this ritual working. You may find a secluded cemetery to use but keep the noise down and be extra careful with any candles or torches, so as to not attract attention or start a fire in the dead leaves.

For this Otherkin Rite of Samhain, you will want to find a cemetery that you can easily get into, at about twilight or just after sunset. This ritual is one of honor to all those that came before us, so each coven member should be in a peaceful and contemplative mindframe upon entering. If you wish, you may try leaving coins at the gate with a short prayer to the spirits of death before entering. If any among the coven have had members of their family or friends that died through the year, you may wish to gather close to their gravesite. Gather the needed items and begin.

Need: 3 Black candles
    1 White candle for each member
    Rattle
    Incense of wormwood
    Smudge Bowl
    Feather fan
    Offerings (candy, tobacco, rum, trinkets, etc)

Find a place close to the graves or between them if you can, and place the three black candles upon the ground in a triangular formation. Place the smudge bowl with wormwood incense between the bottom two points of the triangle. All members of the coven should kneel upon the ground around the triangle of candles and smudge bowl, with the shaman or priest/ess kneeling near the bottom of the triangle. The shaman or priest/ess quiets everyone for a moment of silence, then speaks softly …

"Upon this night of Samhain, we gather here to honor our dearly departed ancestors, family members and friends. Spirits from the other side, hear us and know that we remember you in life and the joys and challenges that we faced together. We call to thee upon this night of Samhain, to give you a chance to speak with us and move into the Otherworld of the spirits of the dead. I ignite these candles that you may find us in the darkness and recognize us as your family, friends, and relatives."

The priest/ess ignites the black candles beginning with the bottom right corner, then the bottom left corner, and finally the top point. After the candles are lit, the priest/ess or shaman ignites the wormwood smudge within the bowl at the bottom of the triangle. The priest/ess speaks again...

> *"I invoke thee, spirits of Death, and ask that you lift the veil before our eyes this night, that we may see with human eyes, between the worlds of the living and dead. I invoke thee, Babael! I invoke thee, Euronymous! I invoke thee, Zagam! I invoke thee into this place between the worlds of the living and the dead! Hear us!"*

The priest/ess or shaman raises the rattle and begins to shake it with a vigorous rhythm and a soft chanting slowly rises from their throat. While the shaman chants, the coven members begin igniting their white candles from the three black candles, burning in a triangle form upon the ground. Each member quietly stills their mind, and thoughts, as the candles illuminate the area between the old headstones. The coven may pass the wormwood smudge around the circle while the shaman chants to empower each person to see within the realms of the dead. If anyone should see anything such as figures or shadows in the darkness moving around the circle of candlelight, try not to get excited or shout out loud, but simply let it be. Wormwood is an herb that is highly aligned with the spirits of the dead and may allow them to rise, especially when hearing shamanic chanting in the cemetery. If the candles should blow out during the rite, have a member of the coven calmly re-ignite them in the same way that was mentioned earlier. Or if you are daring, you may let them all blow out for a moment in the darkness with the spirits of the dead, floating in the night air around you. But be careful and do a proper cleansing upon all members after the ritual. After a time of chanting and rattling, the shaman will slowly let the rhythm fade out. He or she may need a moment to breathe if this has gone on for very long. After a few minutes rest, the shaman or priest/ess of the coven will speak again...

> *"Spirits and daemons of the dead, we thank thee in this night, for this chance to visit again with you in this life. We ask that you accept our humble offerings and find your way into the Otherworld to rest and seek those that have gone before you, as they await your return to the realm of the dead."*

The coven members place their offerings about the cemetery, close to the tombstones and give prayers of thanks and gratitude to any loved ones who are in the area, and beyond. When all return from the offering ceremony, the priest/ess or shaman speaks again, while holding his or her hands out in thanks and welcoming...

> *"We thank thee, daemon keeper and protectors of the cemeteries, Babael! We thank thee sacred*

guide to the realm of death, Euronymous! We thank thee, wild spirit of the crossroads and guide into the darkness at death, Zagam! Hail thee and farewell!"

The coven chimes in after with, "Hail Babael! Hail Euronymous! Hail Zagam!"

The coven will need to leave the cemetery shortly after the rite to keep any wandering spirits from attaching to them. Try to pick up quickly and leave the cemetery as clean or better than you found it. You may go out on the town and converse in a more normal, living place about the events of the evening and ritual. Write any experiences in your journals as soon as you can! Happy Halloween!

Chapter Thirteen
November – Snow Moon

In ancient times, November often marked the time of the first snows of the year. The Snow Moon in this month brings us back to a time of slowed growth and turning inwards to heal and rejuvenate our roots. By this late in the year, all outward growth in plants and life lie dormant, leaves are falling off or are already dead, depending upon where you live. The Snow Moon gives us a chance to look back through the past and into the future, with practices of divination, healing and learning new psychic abilities.

Upon this path of following the moon, we should be in a place at this time of year to be sustained through the winter months, until growth begins again in spring. The harvests of the year are over and unless we must continue to "*hunt and forage*," our projects will survive by growing new roots until their reemergence. For the Otherkin covens, this is a time to journey and practice healing and look into the cycle of the next year for upcoming events, desires and new growth.

Divination practices have been commonplace for Samhain and All Hallows for centuries, but the late autumn and winter months also provide a dark backdrop for the practice and sets the mind in motion for the future. Divination practices seem to be thought of in modern times as ignorant or superstitious, even among people who claim paganism. Divining for answers has been called *"self-fulfilling prophecy,"* by many, but if a good thing is found in the answers of divination, why is this self-fulfilled prophecy bad? Divination practices have been used since very ancient times to foretell events and changes in one's fortune. Even those that *"don't believe"* can be held accountable under the terms and practices of a seasoned practitioner of divination.

Coven Divination

While divination practices are usually a one-on-one scenario, between the reader and the *"client,"* this little working can be performed to see into the future of the coven. If one among you is particularly skilled with a divination set, such as runes, tarot cards, or even scrying, let them perform the reading. If you have a small coven of five or six members, it may be more apt to work than a larger one of ten plus members. Gather the coven together with the necessary items and perform this little divination, to see into the future of the coven.

Need: Divination tool(s) (if a scrying bowl, fill with clean water, or ink, prior to beginning)
   3 black candles
   Small table & chairs
   Dried bluebell flowers (for truth)
   Smudge Bowl
   Smudge wand (sage or cedar)

Be sure to have room around the table for everyone to sit in a chair. This can be around a kitchen table if you wish. Place the three black candles in a triangle around where the divination will be performed. Remember, the reading will be done by the member of the coven with the best ability, which may or may not be the priest/ess of the group. Place the smudge bowl in the center of the table, above the top point of the triangle of black candles.

When all is in place and the table is set, the priest/ess or shaman of the coven will begin by smudging each member of the coven, starting with him or her self. Then the room should be cleansed to remove any negative energy that may impede the results of the working. Now, once everyone and the area have been cleansed, the coven will be seated around the table, with the reader holding the divination tool, or scrying bowl, and seated at the bottom two points of the triangle. At this point, the divination tool is passed from hand to hand around the table three times, with each member asking the same question. Come up with a phrase, such as, *"What is the future for this coven?"*

The coven may also choose to ask a specific deity(s) such as the Norns, Greek Fates, etc., to aid the reading and interpreting the outcome. You may create a spell through this process that will help to guide the energy of the divination tool or set. This can be as simple or complex as your coven is comfortable performing. The following is a Norse based spell calling to the Norns, to aid in a coven divination to see into the future of the coven.

Chant: *"We call upon thee, sacred Norns*
   Urd, Verdandi, and Skuld
   Come to us upon this night
   Let our future be foretold!"

As the chant ensues, the divination tool is passed around the table from hand-to-hand. Before the third time of the chant around the table, the shaman or priest/ess of the group will ignite the candles and the bluebell flowers in the smudge bowl. Passing the divination set between the coven members aids in getting each member's energy into the set, and chanting directs this energy into the reading. (If using a scrying bowl, pass it carefully around the circle before the water is poured into it.) Now, upon the third time around the table, the candles and smudge are burning and the set or tool returns to the reader, who is seated between the bottom two points of the triangle of black candles. The set is *"shook or shuffled"* in the case of tarot cards or runes, or for scrying bowls or mirrors, the hands of the reader may be held over it as in blessing, before the reading. All coven members should be as quiet as possible while the reader works with the divination tool. Runes or tarot cards should be set in a favored pattern and read aloud as to the meanings after all of the placement is made. Runes, can be placed in an *"equal-armed"* or Viking cross, with five runes, to show the past, present and future, as well as above in the mind and below upon the path. The Celtic cross spread for the tarot is quite common and can also be useful in this type of reading. The difficulty falls much on the reader as to interpreting the outcome of the divination, according to the coven or group setting. For a scrying session, everyone should be very quiet until the diviner receives their vision, and can interpret out loud for the coven.

This type of reading for a group can be difficult, but may be well worth the effort, especially when in desire for a long-term coven. Don't let a seemingly negative outcome discourage the members of the group, as this may be something that can be changed for all involved. Remember that in rune reading, it is often understood that the future is not set in stone but determined by our actions, and can be changed by our actions. The runes often foretell the future as a probable outcome, if the same path is followed. Runes can also be read to see if any magick should be worked to help change the outcome discovered. Good luck!

Psychic Abilities Meditation

As the month of November and the Snow Moon are a time of working with psychic abilities and turning inward to grow the roots of the inner self, it would seem beneficial to work with meditations to aid in attaining and strengthening psychic abilities at this time. For the Otherkin coven, a meditation session together can help in strengthening the bonds of the coven, as well as break-up the everyday nuances and boredom of the cold weather.

This meditation is simple and may be a great way of adding to individual strengths and to the coven as a whole. This doesn't have to be any highly decorated ritual working, but in a group setting may require a few items before beginning.

> Need: Five White candles
>   Flour or stones
>   Smudge bowl
>   Mugwort (or other meditational
>   fragrance for incense)

Use the flour or stones to form a circle and pentagram in the center of the gathering area. Make sure the circle is large enough for the coven to sit comfortably around. Place the five white candles at the points of the pentagram and the smudge bowl should be in the center with your favorite meditation incense burning. Ignite the candles from the single top point, around the circle clock-wise or *deosil.* Let the incense smoke envelop the room to inspire the coven to meditation. Let all members be seated and begin counting the breath cycles from one to ten, then starting over. Spend a few minutes of breathing meditation to clear and focus the mind, before continuing. When everyone has had ample time to clear and focus their mind, the priest/ess of the coven may softly ask if *"all are ready."* When everyone signals for ready, the priest/ess begins the chant.

> *Clairvoyant.*
> *Clairaudient.*
> *Clairsentient.*
> *Clairalient.*

The chant slowly builds around the circle, each member chanting in unison. Each coven member should be able to reach a point of only hearing the chant, from their own voice and the voices of those around them. Really try to reach for the still point in the mind during this meditation, as this will further strengthen your abilities. Continue this meditation and chanting as long as you can, perhaps fifteen to thirty minutes, then slowly let it fade. After all coven members have ceased chanting, the candles may be extinguished.

So what does this strange chant do? This is a chant of four of the five psychic senses, beginning with psychic sight, hearing, touch, and sense of smell. The chant is intended to empower each person to pay more attention to and there by empower, his or her own psychic senses. I leave the chant in four as it is easier to get a rhythm for the chant and I don't think I want a psychic ability to taste something as that go wrong in ways I don't even wish to think about. The psychic sense of smell, *clairalience,* can aid the practitioner in following one's nose in situations that *"may not smell right."* This is also linked to many totems as the animals follow their noses to survive, hunting and foraging or simply remaining hidden. Clairalience and its connections are a part of the base or root chakra as a part of survival of the being. The nose is linked to sexual energy and impressions should be attended to when things don't smell right in some situation to us.

Clairsentience, or the ability of *"psychic touch,"* can be used when in contact with an object or person to *"see through their eyes,"* so to speak. This can also be related to "empathy," or picking up on other peoples emotions and feelings. I have tapped into people's memories in this way in the past and this isn't always pleasant, as it requires their emotion to overflow into you. This sort of ability isn't well known but is possible with practice and attention to what we receive in mental impressions. Psychic impressions from an object or person are received with a clear mind and focus of attention on the slightest of knowledge that does not seem to be your own. This again, strengthens the need for the practicing witch or Otherkin to keep a meditation practice and a still mind, or be able to call up that state of a still mind at will.

Clairvoyant ability is the most famous of psychic senses, and is the ability to *"see,"* psychically, or with the mind. Obviously, this requires the practitioner to open the third eye chakra and again use impressions and energy as a guide. Clairvoyance is tied to connections with others, in dream work or astral projection, as well as attaining the sudden vision of what may be to come, a message that isn't seen with the physical eyes, and the like. This sense is opened and strengthened with the *"Om mantra,"* when used in seated meditation. Without straining, close the eyes and look up into the eyelids, while chanting, *"oommm,"* for fifteen to twenty minutes each day. Allow the vibration to help you transcend the flesh and open your psychic sight and intuition.

Clairaudience, is psychic hearing, and actually is connected with the sacral chakra below the navel. This is the source of our *"gut-instincts,"* about a situation and may allow us to *"hear what is not being said,"* as well as what is being said in the physical. Trusting our impressions is highly important to use this sense and keep it in mind, when dealing with this person, or persons again in the future. If we are to develop any psychic abilities we must first learn to trust whatever impressions or gut instincts that we receive.

Just for the sake of knowledge, *clairgustance* is the ability or experience of psychic taste. This one can be tricky but I have had a friend in the past that went through a period with experiencing different psychic senses over a short amount of time. This one stood out in what he told me. We were all young, and sitting around passing a joint, when he began experiencing clairgustance, or psychic taste. He told each person in the room, what they had last eaten or consumed that remained on their breath, without any way of knowing what had gone on earlier in the evening. When he got to me, he said my name, and I replied, *"have a cigarette."* He verified it.

One general term I will discuss here is *"claircognizance."* This term refers to any psychic ability or intuitive perception. The intuition and psychic insight is highly prized or should be, in the magical and spiritual community and all of the above psychic abilities are of the intuition and intuitive faculties. The specific terms give more understanding of how to work with psychic abilities in a specific way, engaging the chakras and opening the senses with a purpose, rather than just waiting around and hoping that we receive a psychic gift. These gifts can come with a price and it is not that they will always be there, so don't take them for granted. Our spiritual bodies are always in a state of change, just as nature is, and we will go through periods of time where one sense is more active and open and then it will slowly fade, allowing room for something else to arise. Psychic abilities and intuitive or mental impressions have to be worked with, strengthened and trusted over time and practice on your path.

I have strengthened my own psychic abilities with this type of meditational chanting and chakra work over time. This practice does not require the practitioner to be in their meditation space for it to work, nor involve a lot of ritual regalia. So long as you can focus and chant, you can even do this with your eyes open. Use this information and meditation practice as often as you like and watch your senses and abilities grow.

Snow Moon Ritual

The rite of the Snow Moon for the Otherkin coven should be one of healing inner wounds for all involved. In honoring the Snow Moon, this gives us permission to relax for a period and release what is not needed, that which is stressing us or aggravating the situation and our life. Not all healing is *"white-light and pretty, pretty,"* as deep healing requires us to face what must be faced, whether we have ran away from it for a year or a few decades. This can be difficult if the practitioner or person being healed isn't ready to face it. Many people say that we face things when the time is right, but in our modern day, this is not always so. More often than not, I have seen people that will find an excuse to ignore the problem, hoping it will go away and they will be free to remain ignorant. This isn't a *"cut-down"* or degradation of the person either, ignorant simply means that we have not been taught, but still have the possibility to learn.

For a rite of the Snow Moon, consider what or who needs to be healed within the coven. If you truly feel and all members agree, that they are in a decent place in their growth and life, then you may wish to perform a generalized healing for the chakras using crystals and/or sound healing modalities. For more intensive work upon an individual in the coven, trust in your intuition and listen to what they have to say about their predicament, while paying attention to your own impressions. Shamanic journey may be used to attain more wisdom and understanding of what is really needed in the healing ritual. Spiritual healing is never a single way, set in stone, as if to go to a doctor's office and receive a medication for the ailment. Healing requires knowledge and understanding, along with a healthy dose of wisdom and compassion.

In this ritual, each member should spend some time and consider what most hinders their growth or causes them the most problems, which can be healed in ritual. Coven members should write down what ails them or create a representation of the ailment to be healed during the rite. If the representation will not burn, such as a clay doll, it can be buried after the ritual is over. All will be ritually burned or destroyed during the rite and then a group journey for healing will ensue, among the coven under the Snow Moon.

    Need: Drum & beater
        Rattle
        Smudge bowl
        Sage or cedar smudge wand
        Blankets to lie upon
        1 black or green candle
        7 quartz crystals
        Flour or stones
        Medicine shield

In beginning this ritual, set up the area with the Medicine shield hanging on a northern wall or if out doors, on a stand in the north. Use the flour or stones to create a circle and draw a seven-pointed star within it. Place a quartz crystal at each point with the point facing inwards to the center of the circle, with a black or green candle in a holder in the center. Remember that black represents death and is the absorption of the negative, or green is a color of the heart and new or renewed growth. Coven members should bring their representations, whether written or created, and lie on the blankets around the circle. The priest/ess or shaman of the coven will smudge the circle with cedar or sage, and then rattle around it, to cleanse away any negative energy. The priest/ess or shaman is seated in the north near the Medicine shield and speaks...

"Upon this night of the Snow Moon, we gather here to be healed of our ailments and sorrows in life. The Snow Moon brings us to a time of turning inward and strengthens our roots, while the snows and cold cover the land. Let us focus our minds on healing and releasing that which holds us back from being whole in this life."

The drumming begins softly in the background, as the priest/ess raises his or her hands to the sky...

"Daemoness Verrine! We call upon thee in this night! Grant us your blessing and energy into this place, that all within may find healing and wholeness. Daemoness of Healing, let your energy and presence be felt by all who attend this rite. Guide us to wisdom and compassion, as we release the sources of our suffering! Hail thee, Verrine! Daemoness of Healing! Come unto us!"

The coven calls, "Hail thee, Verrine!"

The priest/ess or shaman reaches into the circle and ignites the candle in the center and says aloud...

"Sacred flame and source of light
Burn away our sorrows tonight
Release us from our burdens bore
Let our healing be restored!"

He or she then motions for each member of the coven to ignite his or her representations by the flame of the candle burning in the center of the circle. As the representation is ignited in the flame, the coven member says,

"Lady Verrine, Lady Verrine
Grant your blessing unto me!"

As the representation burns, it is placed into a fire-proof container sitting beside the circle. After all coven members have burned away their representations, the shaman speaks again...

"As we remove this representation in the physical realm, so should we go into the Otherworld to complete our healing and speak to the spirits that guide us. Verrine, daemoness of healing, let us claim our right to be whole and healthy in this life. Guide us as we journey to a healing place, to see what went wrong in our life, or what decisions were made that brought us to this place of pain and suffering, that we will not repeat these mistakes and learn our lessons. Hail thee, Verrine!"

The drum begins to beat faster, signaling to the coven that it is time for the journey to begin. Each member should go to their place in the astral to meet their power animal or spirit guide, and let this spirit take them to where they most need to be and what they need to see. These journeys can have an emotional out pouring at the end, so be compassionate to any and all that journey and return with deep emotions. Many times, healing journeys take us to places that are more beautiful than anything we have ever seen, and this by itself can bring about an emotional reaction in many people. After a time of journeying, let the drum call you back. Give thanks to any spirits that guide you or help you in some way before returning to your place in the astral plane and coming back to normal consciousness. Keep a journal near by to write about your experiences.

When all have returned to normal consciousness and recorded their experiences in the journey, the coven may share their experiences with the shaman and among each other. If anyone has emotional issues after the journey, be compassionate, but help them to understand what it is they are feeling, and how to integrate it into their daily life and consciousness. After the sharing is complete, or begins to turn into chatter, the remnants of the representations, can be buried in a small hole, near the gathering area, or at a crossroads if you wish.

Before the rite is ended, the priest/ess speaks once more…

"By the Snow Moon, we have been granted much healing and spiritual experience. Let us give our thanks to all the spirits that guide us, in this world and in the Other realms. We thank thee spirits for all your aid in this ritual of healing. Be

with us in our coming days, to allow all the energy attained here tonight, to be integrated into our lives. Hail Thee, daemoness Verrine! And thanks to all!"

The coven answers, "Hail thee daemoness Verrine, and thanks to all!"

Be sure to take all of the representations to be buried and try to burn them up as much as possible before hand. The rite is over!

Chapter Fourteen
December – Oak Moon & Winter Solstice

Here we are at the last month of the year, and the time of rebirth of the yearly cycle. December's Oak Moon and Winter Solstice give the Otherkin coven a chance to journey into the Underworld, following the sun in its cycle of death and rebirth and is a time to honor the forest spirits, whether we view them as faery, daemon, or deity. The Oak Moon in this month is a time to go within and find our inner wisdom, as we look back over the year and see how things have grown to fruition for our creative and life projects. If we have followed the lunar cycle, we may realize that we feel and view things in a different way than we did at the beginning of the year.

The Winter Solstice is the shortest day of the year and is often celebrated as a time of darkness among vampiric practitioners. This time of year is also the rebirth of the light, as the days grow longer again into the next calendar year. Otherkin covens may also wish to exchange gifts as is customary, make wreaths, honoring the cycle of the Earth's seasons, or decorate a Yule tree in the forest, honoring the spirits therein. There are plenty of opportunities for dark or light magic through the winter months, in the coven of the Otherkin.

Honoring the Forest Spirits

This rite is based in classic pagan/Wiccan rituals and is intended for honoring the spirits of the forest, be they corporeal or purely astral. This hearkens back to a time when people weren't sure that life would continue through the harshness of winter's fury. Our pagan ancestors saw evergreen trees as a sign that life would continue, and began decorating trees in the forest as a way of honoring those spirits. It is from this tradition that we eventually gain the Yule or Christmas tree in modern times.

For this ritual, gather the coven together to make decorations. It will be better to make them by hand from natural items, rather than buying them, as you may not be able to return to retrieve your decorations later or before they are destroyed. We don't want to litter the forest with modern trash, as this happens enough already. Try to use hemp or cotton thread for stringing and tying items to the trees so that we ultimately leave no trash over time. Remember that nylon thread may be strong enough but is basically plastic. Simple things like pinecones filled with peanut butter, rolled in birdseed and tied to the tree branches are ideal for decorations. Strings of popcorn and berries or simple offerings of rice or dried herbs tied in a bundle can also be used. Any other ideas for natural decorations that run in family traditions among the coven can also be shared at this time of year. If you wish to make deity or spirit specific decorations, honoring the gods from the various pagan traditions around the world, you may do this as well. Have fun with creating decorations and put lots of happy and loving energy into it, before the rite begins.

This ritual may be performed before the full moon or around the Winter Solstice, as the weather or your coven's circumstances permit. When you have your decorations ready, go out to a place in the forest where you have gathered before for magic and ritual. Find a cedar or other evergreen tree to decorate that is near your gathering area or on the path going to it. This is where the ritual should take place. As best you can, let all members of the coven circle the tree or gather to the side(s) as is necessary. The priest/ess or shaman of the coven moves to the front of the group and raises the staff out to the forest and speaks...

> *"Upon this day, we gather here to honor the forest spirits as did our ancestors from so long ago. Spirits of the forest, hear us in this rite as we honor the ancient ways of the Earth and its many people. Let us celebrate in the cycle of seasons and the death and rebirth of the Sun in this year. Accept our humble offerings to the forest, animals and spirits, as we among this coven view all life and spirits as divine and beautiful!"*

Coven members may begin to decorate the tree chosen for the offerings and decorations. Let this be something fun and enjoyable, although you may all be cold and miserable due to the weather. Happiness can warm us in ways we don't realize, sometimes just because it distracts us from our misery. Weather permitting, you can play in the snow, build a small campfire or explore some around the forest, seeing what the dead of winter has changed and perhaps revealed within the forest. Winter makes the forest feel different as we can see further between the trees or discover nests and other things that were hidden by them.

When the coven is ready to end this simple rite, the shaman or priest/ess may speak again in closing...

> *"Spirits of the Forest! We give thee thanks and bid farewell upon this day. Accept our offerings to all that dwell within the forest and let us enjoy many more days and nights, of working magic and ritual in this sacred place. May the spirits of the forest prosper through winter's grip and be renewed in the coming year! Hail thee!"*

> *The coven calls, "Hail thee Spirits of the Forest!"*

Be sure to extinguish any fires and pick up anything left over before leaving.

Oak Moon Ritual

The Oak Moon is a time of going within to find wisdom and bring forth a new creation for the coming year. The long winter nights grant us the opportunity to utilize our dark aspects to create in the shadow realms and bring our creations out into the light in the next year. It can require much wisdom to achieve this depending upon what we are seeking in the dark, and how we go about bringing it forth. The following is a meditational rite amongst the Otherkin coven to go within to find wisdom and new creations for the next year of our life.

Before we begin this meditational working, take some time to consider what wisdom or creations you are seeking. Ask yourself some questions regarding your ambitions and goals that have been set in the last few months. Also look at your life situation(s) at the time before the working, as this may provide clues that will help you as well. Do you want to learn something new, to be given a new opportunity or ability for financial or spiritual gains? Do you want to become more devoted to your spiritual or magical path or perhaps devote more time to other interests? These are the questions the coven should be asking themselves for a few days prior to the working. Giving ourselves a few days allows time for certain "coincidences," to give us a sign of what may be needed within our life. This questioning and desiring may have actually begun at the time of the new moon in December and come to fruition under the Oak Moon's full brightness.

Spend a few minutes prior to the working to allow all members of the coven to clear there minds and focus on the ritual. To begin this ritual, first be sure that there will be no visitors or excess noises that will disturb the gathering space. Coven members should be very adept with meditation practices for this ritual to be effective and successful. All you need is a single white candle in the center of the gathering space, with room enough around it for coven members to be seated for meditation. Incense for meditation may be lit within the room to aid in creating the atmosphere desired, but don't let it get too smoky. The priest/ess or shaman of the group may wish to sit in the northern corner, if possible. Be sure that the room temperature is comfortable to allow for deep meditation without the distraction of being too cold. When all is ready, the shaman speaks...

"Upon this night of the Oak Moon, we gather together to seek within our mind and heart, as individuals and as a coven. Let us look within our souls to find what is true for us, and if we can, bring forth new ideas and creations for the next year. Let us be blessed in this night, as we contemplate our lives, our paths and goals and our dreams and visions of our future. Blessed Be to all!"

The coven answers, "Blessed Be to all!"

The priest/ess or shaman of the coven reaches forward to light the single white candle in the center of the gathering space. As it is lit, the gathering area is illuminated from this center point, guiding the way through the darkness of the night. The single candle should be the only illumination in the room from this point on. Each member of the coven begins slow, deep breathing techniques to induce a meditative state of mind. If you wish, the coven may join in a group chanting of a mantra or single tone to begin the meditation and help in inducing the proper state of mind. You may also have one member of the coven to count breathing cycles out loud, to harmonize the breathing and meditation work among the group.

As this state of mind is reached, the coven gathering grows extremely silent and still, seated around the candle burning in the center of the room. This meditation can last for some time if allowed to, so long as there are no distractions or sudden noises from the outside world. I would put some minor time limit on the rite, like an hour to an hour and thirty minutes at most, but you may choose to make it up to the individual as to how long they spend in meditation. Since our meditative ability is often tied to how much we are thinking or distracted, some members may find what they seek within the meditation faster than others, and we should give respect to those having difficulty or that need more time. If members finish the meditation early, they may quietly leave the room to allow the others to finish in silence.

After everyone is done with the meditation, spend some time talking about what was experienced by each person within the coven. Share stories and converse about new wisdom gained or signs and omens that may have been received during the ritual. Remember that it is in understanding our spiritual experiences that we attain new ground and understanding in our life and path. This is the reason for sharing after the ritual is over, so I highly encourage it. Gaining wisdom in these experiences can aid us in the coming days, weeks, months, and even years, but if we disregard it, it will be useless. It is usually in the application of what we learn that makes a difference in daily life. For this time after the meditation, each member is encouraged to take notes in a journal to save and look back over at a later time. Keeping notes on deep meditations can give us a reminder later that we may need to keep us on track.

Winter Solstice Ritual

The Winter Solstice is the last of the year's holidays, not counting the modern New Years Eve, of course. The Solstice marks the beginning of winter and this is the time of going within the Earth, into the darkness of the Underworld and the unknown, before reemerging into the light. People from around the world have long honored many spirits in this sacred time of year. For the Otherkin coven, this may be a time of journeying to the Underworld, to learn from these ancient spirits, no matter how we may view them.

For this ritual, I will use the more generic term of "the Horned One," as many spirits of gift giving are horned or antlered spirits of prosperity, connected to the Earth and forest. You may view this wild spirit as you wish, just replace the name I use here for the rite. Journeying to speak to the Horned One can be somewhat frightening at first, until you sense the energy around him. This is similar to traditional witchcraft and invoking or conjuring the "Devil" or "Black Man," himself for guidance, gifts of power or whatever is needed. Each member of the coven should be prepared mentally and emotionally for this experience and have an understanding of their own views of ancient pagan and earthly spirits. If you have experienced the astral sabbat, earlier in the year, this will have helped you to prepare for this experience. Gather the needed items and the coven and begin.

Need: 5 Black candles & holders
   Flour or stones
   Smudge wand
   Rattle
   Drum & beater
   Horns or antlers (if available)
   Blankets to sit on
   Cedar or pine incense
      (Or your favorite for the holiday)
   Smudge Bowl
   Journals & pens

Create a circle of flour or stones in the center of the gathering area. Make a pentagram in the center with the single point facing north and place a black candle in its holder at each point. If you have antlers or a set of horns available, they can be placed near the top point with the smudge bowl. Make sure the circle is large enough for all coven members to sit on the blankets around it comfortably. Place the smudge bowl with cedar, pine, or your favorite holiday incense near the top point with the candle. The priest/ess or shaman or the coven will first cleanse him or her self with the smudge wand, then each coven member. After each member has been cleansed, the priest/ess or shaman will begin to clear the energy of the circle with the rattle, shaking it vigorously around the circle and chanting...

> *"I cast thee, sacred circle of power*
> *Be focused here, from this hour!"*

After rattling the circle and making three rounds, the priest/ess or shaman will return to the top point to ignite the candles and incense in the smudge bowl. Now the priest/ess sits before the coven at the northern most point and speaks...

> *"Upon this night of the Winter Solstice, we gather here together to honor the spirits of the winter and the forest, as we seek their wisdom for a new year. Let us be clear of mind and heart, as we journey into the darkness of the underworld."*

Drumming begins softly as the priest/ess holds the smudge bowl aloft and speaks...

> *"Tonight, we offer the Horned One this incense of the forest and the Earth. Come to us in this night and join our circle to guide us in your ways. Hear us as we invoke thee Great Horned One, come forth upon cloven hooves and teach us your wisdom for the coming year!"*

The priest/ess billows the smoke of the incense for a moment to fill the room with a light hazy tint, then lifts the rattle again, and begins chanting in harmonious rhythm with the drumbeat. The chant is the *"Song of No Words,"* a chant that comes from the shaman's inner spirit, to interact and make contact with the spirits of the Otherworlds. The shaman or priest/ess of the coven calls one last time...

"Great Horned One, join us in this circle, come and be as our guide into the Underworld!"

The drumbeat slowly becomes more rapid as the coven members close their eyes and the priest/ess or shaman's chanting grows more intense. The journeying begins. Each member should visualize going into their place in the astral as they have done before, to connect with their guides or power animals before journeying further into the Underworld. From their place in the astral realm, they may fly to a cemetery or journey down a hole in the ground and emerge in the Underworld. As we get more adept at journey practice, the spirits may simply put you where you need to go. For this journey, we seek the Dark God or Horned One of the forest to speak to him at his wooden throne in the forest. Stand humble before him and ask your questions about circumstances slowly, giving him time to answer. He may direct you to something that has more relevance in your life than you thought. You may be told to give yourself time or any number of things. Listen carefully to what he tells you and take into consideration that this being does have your best interest at heart, if you will only pay attention and listen.

After a time, the journey will be called to an end. When you hear the call back, let him finish what he is telling you and bid him thanks and farewell before journeying back to your place in the astral realm and slowly opening your eyes. As you come back to normal consciousness, reach first for your journal or notebook to write about your journey. Let everyone return to normal consciousness before giving discussion and closing the ritual. When all are ready, the shaman or priest/ess of the coven may close the circle in their usual way and extinguish the candles before cleaning up the room. Be sure that the coven members have a chance to give their thanks to the Horned One before completing the ritual.

Chapter Fifteen
Otherkin Archetypal Path Workings

For the Otherkin that wishes to learn more about spirituality and magic, a path working may be what is needed. A pathworking is the process of aligning one's self, magically and spiritually with a certain type of energy for a period of time. Pathworkings may last a few months, six months, a year or a lifetime. It depends upon the practitioner's ability to remain devoted to the path and live their life in a way that directly corresponds to the purpose and spiritual alignment of the pathworking. It can require deep dedication to make a pathworking last for many years but it is not entirely unheard of. In giving you the information to help you to decide if a pathworking of the Otherkin persuasion is right for you, I have created here six path workings devoted to different archetypal energies that may be of benefit. You can use this as a guide to learning more about yourself and your spiritual purpose in life as you feel guided to do. The workings here may be used by a solitary practitioner or as rituals of devotion, initiation and progress within a coven.

Modern witchcraft and paganism has worked with archetypal imagery for many years. The idea of an archetype is a psychological model that is most often used in spiritual practices, to give a foundation to many varying deities, beliefs and religions. In working with archetypes we pay attention to our lives and decisions and focus on *"grounding"* the energy of the archetype into our life, thereby becoming as the archetype. Archetypes can range from the subtle aspects of modern people, tied to an occupation, position, or character trait, to the very ancient, archaic and strange. Archetypes may be light or dark, wholesome or chaotic, and more often than not, they have a balance of these aspects within each, being light and dark, good and bad. Some well-known archetypes, such as the "devil" or "tricksters" may be thought of as "evil" in the modern mind, but they embody traits that are necessary for nature to continue, playing a much needed role that mankind simply does not like. Each archetype will have its balance, either within itself, as some aspect or another, or as an equal and opposite being. Don't confuse this with some proverbial, *"battle between good and evil,"* as they are really in balance and harmony, being *yin and yang*.

For the more positive archetypes, the archer or hunter/ ess was once a major part of forest lore and a keeper of that folklore as well as being highly knowledged in herbs and their uses for food or medicine. This archetype has been degraded by modern man due to lack of respect for nature and the desire to conquer rather than work with. The warrior archetype has been replaced with the soldier, another mistake on our part, as it is truly not the same in traits or way of life. The soldier can only follow orders, the warrior decides for him or her self what is right or wrong. The healer archetype is also well known, being wise and compassionate and in their own way powerful, but again has been degraded into some crying, bleeding heart of a figure in our modern era.

There can be as many archetypes as we have traits, occupations and ways of life. If we can simply place each trait into a being that embodies this energy and lives its life in a certain way or under special rules, we have created an archetypal image to follow and learn from. The archetype is the mental aspect of every religion worldwide, as followers look to circumstances to determine which archetype or deity is in power, whether helping or striking out at them. Archetypes are even embodied in the chakras and will dictate how we live our lives and interact with others. These may be internal such as how treat people and work with others, or external, determining our life path. Some examples of internal archetypes in the chakras are the lover, the victim, the martyr, the mother or father, and the Emperor or Empress. These archetypes determine our place in interactions with others and our financial abilities in life. External archetypes more determine a life path, such as the warrior, healer, or a mystic. Some may be considered as both internal and external, depending on the trait and how it is being used. The warrior for example, can stand up to the tyranny of big businesses or wrongful judgments for them selves (internal) or for others (external). The mystic stands between being a teacher of the occult and healing arts, and still being a student and practitioner of magic and shamanism.

The Otherkin practitioner has the opportunity to learn to walk a path of creating our self in this archetypal image. By aligning the self and traits with the character(s) desired, we learn and grow over time of the path working. Keep in mind that the archetypal rituals in this chapter are a means of devoting yourself to the path, which may last a few months, to a year or more, depending upon where your allegiances or devotions truly lie. Within this chapter, I will explore six different popular external archetypes and their corresponding traits, similarities and differences, as according to the Otherkin way of being and believing. Each of these can easily be applied to all practices of the Otherkin, no matter what "kin," or gender you are. Some may be obvious at first glance, but what about your way of doing this? Does every "elf-kin" have to be a hunter? What if your personality is more of the trickster or healer, then what? If you are a dragon, what kind of dragon and what archetype does it fall under? Can a vampire also be a healer or a mystic? What about those of us that can embody many traits from different archetypes, being or becoming true shapeshifters? This is for you to decide.

Many Paths of the Shapeshifter

I will begin this exploration into archetypal figures with the most complex figure that I have worked with. The pathworking of the shapeshifter is one of seeing the many ways in which our lives change and grow in each day. The shapeshifter must learn to "go with the flow," so to speak. A shapeshifter's traits will not remain constant, as we need only accept our abilities and allow our minds and bodies to do what comes naturally. So the shapeshifter is a highly talented and intelligent being, able to transform itself in any situation in life and eventually change their overall life itself. Learning all of the paths here is a good start, as the shapeshifter may at any given time need to be a healer, for someone in need, or a wise one and mystic, to teach others and give advice. Shapeshifters are often considered tricksters, but the energy is just slightly different. A shapeshifter can act and be as the trickster, but will not remain in that energy all the time. Tricksters are often connected with the crossroads and the possibilities in store for us in life. As humans, we tend to think of things in terms of solidity or as one-sided, meaning we think we are only one thing at any given time. It is in this identification with only being one thing that we undermine our possibilities. Ordinary people call upon each other, because they do not learn more than one ability or way of living. The shapeshifter is the "*jack of all trades*," kind of person that changes with the need or territory. The trickster aspect of the shapeshifter may be one of crude jokes and mild tricks to break up negative energy, lead people astray, and hide something or perhaps to defend his or her family without any real fight.

A shapeshifter should be a capable hunter in many aspects of life, as this is another archetype that can be complex. Hunters don't just hunt for food as the path can be applied to anything we seek in life. It is in the application that the shapeshifter learns to be patient, silently stalking its prey (and I don't mean "*stalking*," in a bad way.) Predators use techniques of patience and silent stalking until they are close enough for the attack and kill.

The hunter archetype, even with a skilled shapeshifter, would do well to attain a jaguar, panther, wolf, bear, fox or other such power animal as a totem on the path. The shapeshifter must highly embrace the practices of totemism, learning to interpret signs and omens as well as attaining shapeshifting abilities with many different animal spirits within ritual practices.

There are many totems, spirits and deities that have been linked with shamanism and shapeshifting for centuries. Among the totems that teach shapeshifting, are the crow and raven, fox, coyote, and moose. These are the central totems and energies to contact and work with in learning this sacred occult art. I realize that many people in the Otherkin community identify with wolves and other totems but these do not *teach* shapeshifting, they are just a favored totem or power animal. Remember that in totemism, no one animal is greater or lesser than the others; their energy is just different and needed for different things. One can be a shapeshifter and take on any form but that does not mean the form is central to your being. The wise shapeshifter becomes formless or at least goes without favoritism.

Many of these and other animals are linked with deities that are well known as shapeshifters and these spirits can be contacted as well. Among the most popular are Odin, Freya, Hulda, Morgan le Fey, Lycaon, Hecate, Dionysus, the nymphs, most fairies, and many others. Most daemon spirits from the grimoire tradition are also skilled shapeshifters that may be willing to help you learn the path. Learning can require you to attain the attention and affection from at least one of these spirits and your ability to devote yourself to the path may be a main key.

When devoting our spiritual path and even part of our life to anything, we need to know as much about it as possible before making a commitment. A shapeshifter's path may use many different tools and techniques to attain the practitioner's goals. This may include the bow and arrows of the hunter and the axe as a spiritual weapon of the moon and even healing and magical tools such as crystals, herbs, wands and cauldrons. For the long-term practitioner on this path, the warrior's sword or war hammer may also be needed at times for strength and courage, or to cut through lies to find the truth.

Of course, a shapeshifter's main technique will be the ability to shapeshift, using the spiritual form of different totems but this is not all that is necessary. Shapeshifting requires the ability to keep a still mind and not let worries or emotions, cloud your judgment. This means that meditation is a must upon this path. Serious meditation practice is highly encouraged for walking the shapeshifter's path and being true to it. This gives the practitioner of this path working more freedom to be as they wish in life and go with the flow.

Shapeshifter's Meditation

The following is a meditation that can be practiced for those Otherkin who seek to take upon them selves the shapeshifter's pathworking. I realize that if you have read my first book, *"The Book of Satyr Magick,"* I have already created a *Shapeshifter's Mantra*, but that one invokes more of the darker aspects of the shapeshifter's energy, useful in lycanthropic workings. I will not repeat it here, but give you a different one to work with that invokes more of the positive side of the art. This meditation may be used with the Devotional Rite, seen later in this chapter and as a separate practice for this pathworking.

To begin this meditation, you may wish to ignite candles and incense that are pleasing to you and which help in creating the proper atmosphere conducive to meditation. Remember to shut off phones, TVs, and be sure that you will not be disturbed during your meditation. You may set up any items that are appealing to you on an altar and be seated on a meditation cushion but it is not absolutely necessary. For those that wish, willow, is a sacred to plant to the shapeshifter's practice, and may be burned with mugwort and/or wormwood before or during the meditation. Just don't allow the smoke to become to overwhelming when indoors. What is most important is that you are focused and able to clear your thoughts while chanting the mantra.

Begin with a deep breathing practice to get your blood flowing and increase the oxygen level to the mind. Perform deep breathing until you begin to feel a little light headed then let your breathing return to normal. This practice is important as it helps you to get into the proper state of mind for meditation. After this, begin to count your breathing cycles from one to ten then start over until you reach a state of inner calm. Now begin to chant the mantra and focus your mind only on this mantra.

"I walk the path of the sacred shifter
Able to change within,
I transform my inner and outer life
By formlessness I ascend!"

Practicing with this mantra over time should help you to keep your mind focused on the path of a shapeshifter and help you to realize how much the shapeshifter can change within a short amount of time. Practicing often, twice a day for about fifteen minutes in each session is suggested.

Shapeshifter's Devotional Rite

If you wish to take upon yourself this pathworking, you will want to perform a ritual of devotion to the path, as a sort of initiation and a ritual to show your progress in magical and spiritual arts. This rite can be performed as a solitary practitioner or in a coven, if you are a member of one. You will want to use some tools for this rite of devotion to your pathworking. The ritual axe presented here, is a sacred tool of the shapeshifter's path. The curve of the blade represents the crescent moon from which we gain our power and an axe can be used for many things in the forest of the shapeshifter. From battle to hunting or cutting herbs and wood, the axe is a highly adaptable tool, just as the shapeshifter that uses it.

You may wish to purchase a small camp axe and decorate it with leather or carve runes and symbols into the handle that hold spiritual meaning for you. When you are finished with the decorum, create a rite of blessing this sacred tool before using it in ritual. You may also wish to set a time frame such as three months or a year, before beginning the ritual. If you feel you are still on the path or want to continue after this time, you can perform the rite again. This ritual can be performed when we feel ourselves slipping from the path, as well. Our modern society pushes and pulls us in so many different ways it is easy to become lost, overwhelmed or lose our drive for spiritual purpose and empowerment. Gather the needed items and begin.

    Need: Crushed willow leaves
      Ritual Axe
      Flour or stones for circle
      Small pouch or medicine bag (with long leather or thread to tie around your neck, 2"x2" pouch is fine)
      Smudge Bowl
      Pentacle disc (if available)
      Lighter or matches

To start off your rite of devotion, be sure that you have enough willow leaves to use for both a part of a medicine bag and some for the smudge bowl as incense. Go to place in the forest if you can to begin the rite. Make a circle with flour or stones that is large enough for you to sit within and have some space all the way around you.

This may be about four to five feet in diameter. Place the smudge bowl on the pentacle disc in front of you and pour some of the crushed willow leaves into the bowl. Have your Ritual Axe at your side and the medicine bag near the smudge bowl, also on the pentacle disc. Ignite a small amount of willow leaves in the smudge bowl and waft the smoke over you while chanting the Shapeshifter's Meditation Mantra.

> *"I walk the path of the sacred shifter*
> *Able to change within*
> *I transform my inner and outer life*
> *By formlessness I ascend!"*

Chant this mantra until you feel yourself growing more silent from within. Let your mind focus on this mantra to bring yourself to a still point, mentally. Now lift the medicine bag and begin to place some of the crushed willow leaves into the pouch and hold it over the smoke while still chanting. After a minute or two of this, you will state your intent such as…

> *"I seek to walk the path of the shapeshifter,*
> *I devote myself in mind, body and spirit!*
> *For the next three months (six months, a year, etc.)*
> *I dedicate my life and magic to this path!*

Now, hold the pouch in your hands and begin to charge it with your energy, feeling the current flow through you and into the medicine bag. When you feel you have charged this pouch enough, you may hang it around your neck and lift the Ritual Axe. Raise this mighty blade and turn to the eastern corner of the circle. Stand strong and clear your mind. Hold the Axe aloft and call...

"By the axe, I call to the East, Spirits of the Air, and the dawn of new beginnings! Unto the East I call, as I begin a new path as a Shapeshifter. Let the light shine upon this day and aid me in understanding as I walk this path anew! Hail Thee!"

Turn now to the south and raise the Axe again...

"By the Axe, I call to the South, Spirits of Fire, and the powers of illumination and courage. Let me be strong upon this path and walk with wisdom in the ways of the Shapeshifter! Let the fires of strength burn within me, as I walk upon this new path! Hail Thee!"

Turn now to the Western corner of the circle and raise the Axe and call aloud...

"By the Axe, I call to the West, Spirits of Water and Death! Hear me upon this day as I devote myself to the ways of the Shapeshifter! Let my intuition be strong, still my emotions and guide me with inner perceptions upon this path, as I devote myself to the ways of the Shapeshifter! Hail Thee!"

Now turn to the Northern quadrant of the circle and raise the Axe high...

"By the Axe, I call to the North and the Spirits of the Earth! By the powers of the Earth Mother, be as the foundation for my growth and wisdom. Hear me as I walk upon the path of the Shapeshifter and renew my spiritual dedication. Be with me in my days and nights, with strength, courage, intuition and wisdom. Guide me now on this path I walk. Hail Thee!"

Now stand in the center of the circle, and raise the Axe to the sky...

"By the Axe I call to the Spirits of the Sky, You who oversee all of mankind, Hear me! Guide me with the inner perceptions and wisdom of the Shapeshifter, as I change within my path on Earth. Guide me as I walk this path anew! Hail Thee!"

Bend to one knee and hold the Axe before you and call...

"By the Axe and the Earth beneath my feet, I ground this working into my life. Let me walk the path of the Shapeshifter for this time, and until I feel another change is needed. Guide me upon this sacred path! Hail Thee!"

Stand for moment and still your mind, and hold the Axe close to the center of your chest and speak solemnly...

"By the Axe, I walk the path of the Shapeshifter, ever closer to my heart and soul, as I realize my true self within. I am a Shapeshifter! Hail Thee All and Thank you!"

You may sit in meditation for a few minutes after the rite is done. Burn the rest of the willow in the smudge bowl before leaving and pour the ashes upon the ground near where the ritual took place. (Be sure that they are extinguished.) Keep the pouch with you as a reminder and as a medicine bag to attain the spiritual wisdom of the Shapeshifter that dwells within. You may use the Axe in other rituals or keep another one for throwing if you work with warrior practices while on the Shapeshifter's Path. Study your totems well and practice shamanic journey, if and whenever you can. Make prayers to the animals you see for guidance, wisdom and energy. Meditate often to keep a clear mind.

There is one particular challenge I would like to mention to this path and that is, as I said, the mind's identification with one thing or another. As a shapeshifter, we must remember that we are not any "one thing," but many things compiled to make a whole being. We are the sum of all the parts, and this can be hard to wrap our heads around at first. There will be times upon this path that we encounter doubts or thoughts regarding, *"what this path is about,"* and *"what we should or shouldn't be or do."* You can still do the things you love, be loving, strong, independent, etc; but this path requires us to be true, most importantly. Become formless in your mind and the negative thoughts will subside.

Path of the Hunter/ess

The pathworking of the Hunter/ess is very special, as it is one of our most ancient of archetypes. When ancient peoples were gathered in *"hunter/gatherer tribes,"* is when this archetype began. The Hunter/ess archetype will often have more complexity to it than we may realize at first glance. This archetype doesn't just hunt, they must survive by their wits and wisdom in the forest, where the law of the land may turn to *"kill or be killed."* A Hunter/ess must know the lay of the land, be self-sufficient in many aspects of life and know how to forage for herbs and plants to supplement their dietary needs. This can require us to be willing to eat things that ordinary people wouldn't even consider. Hunters live by the ways of the forest and this takes us away from the seasonal rites of the harvest and plunges us back farther in time. To know the seasonal cycles of plants growing in your area can be difficult, if not trained by someone that specializes in this skill. This archetype demands the Hunter/ess be skilled in herbalism as well as archery and ancient techniques of forestry and tracking.

The forest tribes may have been among the first to watch the movements of the animals during weather changes as well as seasonal changes. This is where totemism officially begins. Knowing the animals, their habitats, food sources, traits and patterns of mating and migration, as well as techniques to hunt them efficiently without over hunting is highly important to this path. If the hunter's tribe over hunted, they were forced to move to new land for another food source. This could cause tribal disputes over territories and rights to hunt.

For the Otherkin, this is a path that takes you away from all that is safe and secure in the city, forcing you to live, at least part time, in or near the forest. The Hunter/ess as a pathworking may even require more than the other archetypes written here. Learning and practicing techniques of archery is highly suggested for this pathworking. Even if you don't hunt seasonally for food, a practice of archery or knife/axe or spear throwing can benefit you in bringing this archetype to life within you. Tools and weaponry are a big part of this pathworking, just as the meditations to learn silence and stillness from within. Why would the hunter, armed with a bow and quite capable of using it, need to learn meditation and silence? Because even the most skilled animals don't always get their meal. If you are anxious, bored or mentally distracted, you may miss your opportunity for a shot, thereby missing your next meal. Spirituality can be applied to every path in the world, if we simply put it to use. I won't claim to be some expert or long time archer or axe thrower, but I can tell you that I always shoot better when my mind is focused on the goal, or target, as it were and meditation is a great asset to this.

Many predatory totems would be of the most benefit on the path of the Hunter/ess. Jaguars, cougars, or any member of the cat family, bears, wolves, foxes, and even some insects and reptiles such as the snake or praying mantis can be of aid to the hunter archetype. The thing to think about here is what *are* you hunting? This is where again the application of the spirit's abilities is important. Totems like the praying mantis teach stillness and patience during the hunt, silently waiting for the opportunity. The cat and all members of the feline family have amazing stalking abilities and the ability to remain unseen or heard. This silent stalking ability can be mimicked in ritual to aid in your own practices and hunting. The wolf, more often than not, hunts in a pack, as this allows the wolves to go after larger prey than when alone. This too, should be considered when hunting or practicing. The fox is known for hunting mice, rabbits and other small animals and calling upon the fox's energy may even help you to camouflage or remain hidden. Some of the strange techniques of the fox may also help you with your love life, if applied correctly.

The Hunter/ess archetype has many deities and spirits connected with it that can also be of benefit. Odin, Skadi, Skogsfruar, Holler, Artemis, Diana, Faunus, Apollo (as a god of archery) and even Pan can be connected with hunting, although Pan is commonly identified with flocks and fields. In the grimoire tradition, the daemon Lerajie (or perhaps spelled, Leraie) is a daemon that can aid in learning archery. Making contact in ritual or meditation and working with one or more of these spirits may aid you in attaining the archetype of the Hunter/ess with more wisdom and knowledge of the path.

Hunter/ess Meditation

For this meditation, you may wish to have your bow, spear or other such tool with you, as it is of a primary focus on this path. Other tools are optional for the meditation, as I will repeat; the important part of meditation is the focus of your mind. If you feel a need for items to help you change the atmosphere of your room or space, then you may do so. I have not found any particular herbs that can be used to aid the hunt, aside from those that help to increase the psychic and intuitive abilities, i.e., mugwort, wormwood, eyebright and the like. If you want to burn candles, I would choose a color that represents the season such as green for spring or summer and brown or black for fall and winter. You may even use white to represent winter snow. You can research and align your items with any deities of the hunt that you are connected with or that you desire to contact, in hopes of attaining a sign from one of them.

Clear your space of any items that are not needed before beginning the meditation. Have your Hunter's tool such as a bow and one arrow, a spear, etc; placed on the floor or ground in front of you. You may hold this tool in your hands if you wish, instead of holding a mudra, or hand position during the meditation. Be seated on your meditation cushion or a pillow and relax yourself with some gentle deep breathing practice. Remember to only use the deep breathing until you feel a little light headed, then let your breathing return to normal. Count your breath cycles from one to ten, then repeat this for a few minutes until your begin to feel yourself becoming more clear minded and focused. Listen between the thoughts for silence from within your mind. Now begin to chant the mantra for the archetype of the Hunter/ess and continue this for the duration of the meditation session.

> *"I walk the path of the sacred Hunter*
> *I am the bow and*
> *The arrow that flies through the air*
> *I am the target that it strikes.*
> *I am the silent one of the forest.*
> *I am the Hunter!*
> *I am the Hunter!"*

This meditation mantra is a more of series of affirmations that directly correspond with the art of archery of the Hunter. While many archers today have begun to use modern technology to aid their skills, it is the Hunter of old that has the real ability with the bow. The archer that must shoot with the intuition, rather than a mechanical sight mounted on their bow will appreciate this meditation. The practice of *Japanese Kyudo* or "Way of the Bow," intends the archer to use meditation to *"be the arrow,"* within the mind so that the archer and the bow and arrow become inseparable in spirit. Practice in this art has shown me that it is in the focus of the mind that the archer begins to feel as though their thoughts guide the arrow to its target. This is an amazing feeling for the archer and a strong connection to your art and archery.

You may wish to change or replace a line of this mantra to suit your needs. Adding the phrase, *"I am the spear that flies through the air,"* if you wish or if you use spears as throwing weapons on your path. Affirmations are simply positive statements that if used properly, will aid the practitioner in many things and they aren't difficult to create. Continue to chant this mantra/ set of affirmations for fifteen to twenty minutes during your meditation session and practice often.

Hunter/ess Devotional Rite

In devoting yourself to the path of the Hunter/ess, it is important to realize that it requires much learning. If you remain on this path for a long period of time, you may wish to take a class in herbalism or study sustainable forestry for a long period of time. On top of this, is your practice with weapons, such as bows, spears or throwing knives, etc., which should be taken seriously and practiced often. Be sure during all of this that you are able to keep your mind clear and your heart open for those that you must hunt, as this is a sacred act for an animal to give its life for yours to continue.

For this Ritual of Devotion, you will need to have your sacred tool(s) for hunting with you for the rite. If you shoot a bow, have one arrow with you or just keep them in a quiver on your back or at your side. If it is a spear or other throwing weapon, you may wish to perform a cleansing and blessing over it with a smudge wand, before the ritual begins. Other tools such as a bowie knife that you use when hunting or cleaning the kill, or an axe for cutting wood or throwing may also be cleansed and blessed as a part of the rite. People of the forest need tools to survive, so don't be ashamed of using these in magical rites.

After you have decided which tools or weapons to use, and have performed a cleansing and blessing over them, it is time to begin the ritual devotion. If you have a particular deity or spirit that you work with, look up corresponding herbs, oils or candles to burn or make offerings with during the rite. Totem fetishes or representations may also be a part of this working as your power animal may be your best ally when hunting or journeying through the forest. With this in mind, gather the needed items and dedicate your self to the path of the Hunter/ess.

Need: Totem fetish
   (small bits of fur, claws, a pendant, etc.)
Deity items (herbs, oils, candles, images)
Weapon or tool of choice (bow, spear, etc)
Flour or stones
Wand or staff
Smudge wand (sage or cedar)
Smudge bowl
Offerings and dish (if needed)
Lighter or matches

If possible, perform this rite in a clearing in the forest. If you really wish, you may begin this pathworking on or around Samhain, the seasonal time sacred to the hunter/ess. After you have cleansed and blessed your sacred tools, begin to create a large circle with flour or stones making certain that it is large enough for you to sit in with your tools. Facing north in the circle, place your smudge bowl in the center with any candles on either side. If you are using an image of a deity, you may place it behind the smudge bowl from you, so that the incense smoke will rise in front of it. Your totem fetish may be laid before the right candle and the offering dish on the left. Your sacred weapon can lie across your lap or be laid directly in front of you. When you have your altar tools set up, you may cast the circle using the wand or staff.

Pointing the wand toward the ground, or alternately, pointing the tip of the staff at the ground around you, begin to walk a slow circle while chanting...

> *"I cast this sacred circle of power*
> *Be focused here from this hour!"*

Walk the circle three times while chanting to empower the circle. Now return to your seat in the center facing the north. Strike a match or lighter and ignite the candles, starting with the left...

> *"I ignite this candle to illuminate my path as*
> *a hunter."*

After lighting both candles and saying this with each one, ignite the incense in the smudge bowl and begin wafting the smoke over you while saying...

> *"Let me be blessed upon the path of the Sacred Hunter/ess! Let the spirit guide me to my goals with success."*

Offer the smoke of the incense to the image if you have one, or hold it to the sky and repeat the blessing above. You may create a prayer in your own words to speak to your chosen deity of the Hunt, while wafting the smoke over you and their image. After you have repeated this a few times, lower the smudge bowl back into its place and lift your totem fetish in your hand and speak a prayer in your own words to your power animal or helping spirit, something like...

> *"Spirit of the Fox, teach me your wise ways as a Hunter. Let me attain your stealth and speed, your cunning and agility. Grant me your blessing as I walk this Sacred Path. Hail Thee!"*

Feel your energy charge this fetish item with your energy. Feel it combining with the energy of the animal it represents or came from. Let your energy merge for a moment with this animal spirit. Place the totem fetish back in its place upon your altar. Now lift your weapon or tool of choice. Raise it to the image of the deity, then to the fetish item on the altar. Now hold it high above you and speak aloud...

"As I walk this sacred path of the Hunter, I claim this as my sacred weapon and tool of the path. Let me never be without this sacred tool of the Hunt, for as long as I shall walk this path. By the spirits and ancestors before me, hear my voice. I devote myself to this sacred path, to rise as a Hunter/ess of the Forest. I devote my spirit, mind and body to this path. Hail Thee! Let me walk in new ways in the world! Hail and thank you!"

Hold you sacred tool down to your heart and whisper a private blessing to it. Give this tool or weapon meaning in your life and it will repay you with many great gifts. You may lower your tool back to the ground before you and meditate for a time on this path and ritual. Chant the Hunter's Mantra or affirmations for a time over your newly created sacred tool of the Hunt. Be sure to give thanks before closing the circle and cleaning up. Remember to keep the totem fetish with you, in a pouch or kept near your bed. Keep your sacred tool cleaned and use it often, as you walk this path of the Sacred Hunter/ess archetype.

The Warrior/ess Path

I know that most people only think of the warrior archetype as an ignorant brute, but this is because of our inclination to believe what we see on TV. The true warrior/ess archetype is one of standing strong in the face of adversity and for the proper reasons. The warrior has a difficult task of being compassionate and understanding, along with being willing and able to destroy as necessary. This means that the warrior must connect his or her heart and mind in a clear, seamless whole. The warrior is the archetype of the solar plexus chakra and purified energy is its driving force. The solar plexus works to transform the red, raw, uncontrolled energy of the root or base chakra and the orange, creative and sexual energy of the sacral chakra into a higher vibration, before this energy reaches the heart. The solar plexus, as suggested by it name, is ruled by the sun and its color is yellow. This archetype is highly projective and very masculine in its energy, although the female warrioress is often the epitome of balance between feminine beauty and masculine strength. The warrior is also a path for those with predator totems such as the wolf, bear, cougar, tiger, etc.

Warrior totems are among the most powerful of animals and most commonly known totems. Everyone wants the biggest, strongest, fiercest totem for his or her power animal, but this may not be needed. Other totems such as the deer, elk, elephant or moose may also be useful as warrior totems for their strength, speed, and stamina. It is not entirely necessary to be a predator to walk the warrior path, but is more likely due to the aggressive and predatory nature of the animal. Even some smaller animals such as the wolverine, mongoose, or badger could be easily adapted as warrior totems for their many skills and strengths. The wolverine's ferocity among tribes of the North was near legendary, as this smaller animal could even defend itself successfully against bears. The mongoose may seem odd as a totem but this animal spirit may be the epitome of the vampire-hunter, as it seeks out "snakes" and other prey. The snake or serpent is a well-represented, vampiric totem and this makes the vampire hunter, a warrior with a different cause. The badger as a totem is the storyteller and keeper of stories, and most people like to hear a good battle story as tribute to the warrior in all of us. This makes the badger totem more bard-like when it combines the paths of warrior and teller of tales.

The purpose of the warrior path working is to channel the energy of your totem into your practices for greater strength, endurance and victory in life's battles. The many totems of the warrior will have different ways of manifesting within you and may teach you ways in which the warrior path is more than you expect. The more adept you become at raising this energy quickly for use and then dissipating it so as to not get out of hand, the more capable you will be in attaining your own victories.

The warrior as an archetype has much in common with the athlete, as tests of strength and skills were common among warrior clans. Athletes and warriors in some ancient cultures were one and the same, depending upon their state of affairs with other countries. This makes the athlete archetype as part of the warrior's time-off, or archetype during peacetime and training, while the contests between warriors were entertaining for others in the clan.

Another aspect of the warrior path working is the practice of spiritual tattooing. Many tribes around the world have required that the young warrior attain a tattoo before being considered a warrior, or sometimes even an adult. Spiritual practices for the attainment of a tattoo may be considered for Otherkin practices and covens as well. It is possible to tattoo images of power animals, personal or occult signs and symbols, Otherkin images of the "other-self," and many other designs by the hand of a skilled tattoo artist. For practices leading up to the attainment of your tattoo, these may include tests of strength or mental and psychic abilities, attainment of a power animal, certain ritual initiations, etc. Many aspects can be considered when working with spiritual tattooing, just be sure that the image is something you will be proud of for the rest of your life. Something else to consider is about the actual process of receiving the tattoo. I have been into tattooing for many years and while I'm not covered yet, my experiences with different tattoos have led me to understand a few things to form my own belief about it. If you receive a tattoo with ease and little to no pain or burning sensations during the work, you were more than ready for the tattoo you received. However, if much pain and suffering accompanies a tattoo that you receive, you were not ready, but will be made to attain what you need through the spiritual aspect of the tattoo, now embedded in your skin. If you ever get light-headed, faint or "pass out" during or just after a tattoo, pay attention to any signs, sounds or images that come to you psychically in this in-between state of being. I have had information sent to me a few times during the body shock after a tattoo session and I couldn't have received it without the experience.

Warrior/ess Meditation

There are as many ways to approach this pathworking, as there are different types of warriors. Each warrior stands for a purpose and to attain success and victory for their cause. This can be applied to all of our battles in life, daily stresses or long-term projects. The culture the warrior resides will often determine the type of warrior we are. This may be according to your magical tradition or the physical family heritage and bloodline. The Japanese samurai are vastly different from the Norse, Native American or African tribes of warrior peoples throughout history. The methods of a particular culture may present themselves within your practice. The warrior archetype is about perseverance and determination, but they must also keep a heavy dose of wisdom, near by. This archetype can be applied to many other titles and archetypes that people live within everyday. The office worker that stands up against an unruly boss, condition or rule is still essentially embodying the warrior archetype, having the courage to do what is right. The priest that walks the warrior path teaches and encourages empowerment of mind, body, and spirit. It is through the spiritual alignment and techniques that the warrior-priest attains the self-discipline to spiritually and physically achieve more in their life. From activism to the fight circuit, a martial arts teacher to defense lawyers, the warrior archetype is very much alive today. While our modern society thinks of the warrior in terms of bloody battles or excessive aggression, the truly victorious warrior can be a hero in the end.

There are many ways to practice meditation, especially for the warrior archetype. Moving meditations and exercises such as Tai chi, (with or without a sword,) Qigong, yoga, or any strength and combative training can be used or applied to this archetype's practice of meditation. For the purposes of this book, I will give a more basic meditation of chanting and working on the mental aspects of the path, letting you find your own physical training or exercise practices. For this meditation you will want a quiet space that you will not be disturbed. If you have chosen a weapon to work with for the teachings of this path, then have it available also. You may set up your meditation space to suit your needs or desires. Having a candle to focus on, especially yellow, orange, or red can help with chakra work during the meditation, or you can simply use a white or black. With your warrior's weapon of choice in hand, seat yourself in front of this candle and take a few deep breaths to clear your mind. Remember, to let your breathing return to normal when you feel a little light-headed. Begin to count your breath cycles from one to ten and repeat, letting your mind grow silent. Now hold the tool up in front of you. If you have a sword or spear, you may lay it across your lap and place both hands upon it. If you have an axe or hammer, you may stand them up on the handle, having the blade or head just beneath your hand. Let this be your mudra or hand position for the meditation, your hand, nobly resting on the item. Now as you are counting your breathing cycles, clear your mind and begin to create an image of your Otherkin self or as your animal/humanoid self. See yourself in this form in your mind's eye, seated in your meditation. Begin to feel as though this spirit's energy is coursing through you, as if it is overlaid upon your physical form. Let this visualization grow stronger, feeling as if you are that human-animal hybrid figure seated in meditation. Try to hold the visualization as you chant…

> *"I walk the path of the sacred warrior*
> *With wisdom, courage and might,*
> *By the way of the sacred (<u>weapon</u>),*
> *I walk in shadow and light!"*

Fill in the blank space with the name of your weapon such as sword, spear, axe or hammer. Hold this visualization and chant for as long as you can. Try to perform this meditation twice a day for as long as you walk the warrior's path. This can be a precursor to weapons practice, to help focus your mind on the target and energy of the warrior. This visualization can also help you in attaining a deeper connection with your power animal and you may begin to see more of its traits in your daily life.

Warrior/ess Devotional Rite

For the Otherkin or witch that wishes to become devoted to the path of the warrior, you will want to research or know your patron and/or matron deity or totem. This divine spirit or being is your guide, teacher, and mentor in the pathworking of the warrior spirit. This adds the spiritual and religious element to the pathworking that can help the practitioner in maintaining balance between excess aggression and more noble assistance. The warrior gods, goddesses and totems of ancient pagan traditions can instill a sense of nobility and encourage the proper use of strength and power upon this path.

Because I cannot write a ritual for everyone here, I have created a generalized ritual that can be altered or applied to any path. You can make adjustments for the likes or dislikes of your matron or patron deity or totem. As a part of a witch's or Otherkin coven, this rite can be performed to empower the witch or Otherkin when they need to activate the strength, courage and power of the warrior spirit within them. Create spells or rituals of the warrior's path with the herbs and stones listed on the following page. This list is by no means complete and you may research further if you need.

Courage: yarrow, thyme, tea, mullein

Strength: Saffron, mugwort, bay, thistle

Power: dragon's blood, orange, jasmine, orchid, ginger, devil's shoestring

Victory/ Success: Allspice, Cinnamon, bamboo, pepper, patchouli, sandalwood,

Stones: bloodstone, flint, citrine, garnet, ruby, iron in any form,

Need: 2 red or purple candles
    Weapon of the Path
    Totem Fetish item
    Medicine shield (if available)
    Deity items
    Smudge bowl
    Pentacle disc
    Lighter or matches
    Flour or stones

Herbs and stones from the list above of your choosing for empowerment during the ritual. I would try to obtain one or two herbs from each listing for a more balanced blend of courage, power, strength, and victory. You may choose to blend them together before the ritual takes place, or only take a small amount of each to mix during the rite. Choose a stone to empower during the ritual and keep it with you.

To begin this ritual, clear a large space in a room or go outdoors to a location that you will not be disturbed. Place your tools in the center of the area, as this space will be as your altar for the ritual. Set up the candles to the right and left sides of the space with the smudge bowl and herb mixture in the center, resting on the pentacle disc. You may wish to hang the Medicine shield in front of you on a tree branch or wall, as an emblem of your power animal and its energy. Your totem fetish item and any deity items can be placed before the candles to the right and left of your altar space. When your altar space is set up, begin to mark a circle with flour or stones around the area and empower with your ritual weapon by pointing the end toward the ground and projecting your energy through it while chanting…

> *"I cast thee sacred circle of power*
> *Be focused here from this hour!"*

Walk the circle three times chanting and pointing the end of the instrument to the ground, while you visualize a bright blue circle of energy surrounding this area. When you have completed the third circle, place your weapon back near the altar area. Now ignite the candles starting with the left and give a blessing or intent like…

> *"By sacred light, I illuminate my path as a warrior!"*

After both candles are lit, if you have not yet mixed the herbs, now is the time to begin. However if you pre-mixed them before arriving, you may pour the herb mixture into the smudge bowl and begin to empower them with a chant of your own creation. Something like…

> *"By these sacred herbs aligned*
> *Their power within is now as mine!"*

When you have empowered these special herbs and are satisfied with the energy, you may ignite the herbs and waft the smoke over you to empower your self. Lift the smudge bowl from the pentacle disc and offer to the image of your deity or to the sky and speak...

> *"I offer thee, of sacred herbs,*
> *To walk the warrior's path*
> *Guide me with your wisest ways*
> *Of strength and power that last!"*

Waft the smoke over you and offer again the herbs to the image, then place the smudge bowl back upon the pentacle. Lift the fetish item of your totem and hold it in your hand, feeling the power of this animal beginning to run through you. Hold the fetish in the smoke from the smudge bowl and speak aloud a prayer or blessing of your own creation, something like...

> *"Spirit of the wolf! I call upon thee, be as my*
> *guide and mentor upon the warrior path. Let my*
> *wisdom be matched by my strength and cunning,*
> *and let my ferocity be feared by my enemies. Grant*
> *me the perseverance and willpower of the warrior,*
> *to walk with wisdom and might! Hail thee!"*

Hold the fetish for a moment feeling its energy running through you. Shapeshift in your visualization, becoming the zoomorphic form, kneeled before your altar. Hold this visual image for a few minutes then, place the fetish back upon the altar. Now, raise the stone that you have chosen to empower and create a blessing over it while holding it in the smoke. Empower this stone with your energy, imbuing it with the powers you seek. Hold it in your hand and breathe a long breath of power into it, feeling the energy flowing from your core into this stone. When you are finished, place the stone back upon the altar. Finally, you lift the sacred weapon of your path and raise it to the sky. Hold this weapon in your hands for a moment, then hold it over the smudge bowl and allow the smoke to purify it, as you speak in honor of the weapon you have chosen. Hold the weapon in one hand, and hold the other in blessing over it and speak...

> *"By this sacred sword, I live, to walk in the warrior's way. With courage and perseverance, with strength and might, I bless this sacred steel. Aid me in cutting through the lies to find the truth in all things. Let the flash of my blade strike fear in the hearts of those that would take my rights or life. Let me stand strong for those that cannot. I stand for the truth and freedom, in all ways. Hail thee, to the spirits of the warrior of ancient times. Hail thee to the warrior spirits not yet born. Let us rise to victory and glory. Hail thee!!"*

Sit in meditation for a time in reflection upon your new path. You may wish to perform some deep breathing and empower the solar plexus chakra with visualization. You may meditate on warrior ancestors, or tribes and their ways. Spend some time considering this path and the many ways in which the warrior stands for what they believe in. The weapon is a reminder of the path you walk and remember that a good warrior stands for those in need. When you are ready, give one final thanks to the spirits and totems that guide you, then close the circle and pack up your tools.

You may use this weapon in warrior practices to continue the empowerment of the path. Be sure that you use it wisely in physical respects and be careful of others.

The Healer's Path

The Healer as an archetypal pathworking is one of the gentlest and yet more difficult of paths, as the healers must first heal themselves of emotional and physical distress before healing anyone else. Much of this pathworking aligns with the use of color, light and sound, to align the chakras for deep meditations and spiritual energy. The true healer of this pathworking must realize that there are times we need to go through our difficulties or face our fears, in order to learn from our earthly walk. The healer most often provides the place and energy for healing to take place, as spiritual healing is not a forced affair, as in modern medicine. A gifted healer can aid in the relief of pains and emotional distress only if the patient or client is willing and able. This requires effort, understanding and desire from the patient as well as the knowledge of the healer to guide them. The Healer therefore, becomes a provider of guidance, wisdom and sacred space for all that come to them.

For the Otherkin or witch that wish to walk this path, there are a variety of totems, spirits and teachings to guide you on the way. Among the natural healing totems are the butterfly, dragonfly, hummingbird, ladybug, and dolphin. These are special totems of the light that work at the level of the chakras, aiding us in raising our vibrations to a higher state to allow for the flow of healing energy. While there are effective healers that have other totems such as tigers, wolves, and serpents, these are among the gentler totems that stand out and more highly populate the metaphysical and healing field.

This can also be a great path for those of the water element, both in totems and as an Otherkin, i.e., mer-folk, dragons, etc. Water has long been a keeper of the secrets of life, healing knowledge and power and for those that wish, you may commune with the water elemental of your choice for deeper learning and energy. For the serious practitioner of this path, there are also many herbs and oils for use and a variety of energy healing therapies to learn as you grow upon the Healer's path.

The tools of the Healer archetype are vast in range and are often chosen according to the healer's tradition, interests or practices. Any number of crystals and stones, herbs, oils, colors, symbols and musical instruments can be used in healing rituals and spiritual therapies that exist around the world. Healers are often gifted at divination as well and may even be as spiritual teachers, depending upon their calling. Divination and teaching are often overlooked in the healer's path, as we think of doctors in modern times, giving medication and sending us on our way. The healer must teach the patient how to overcome their obstacles from within, allowing time for the patient to become healthy, balanced and whole again. Healing such as this can require any number of divination readings as according to the divination tools used by the healer. Tarot cards, runes, bones or any other divination tool that you are interested in or work with already can be used for gaining information before and after the healing is performed. This position of being a diviner and healer aligns this path with that of, the priest or holy man or woman. The priest or priestess may be a shaman or shamanic practitioner as well, but it is not always necessary. While shamanic practice is recognized in healing, the healer doesn't have to be a shaman to be effective. It is in the ability of the healer to channel energy through symbols, chants and other tools that determines the effectiveness of the ritual. To align with this sacred intent and energy requires the healer to attain the intensive focus of the mind that is gained in meditation.

Healer's Meditation

For the path of the Healer, meditation is of utmost importance. The healer's path is highly spiritual and harmonious, often seeking to attain balance and enlightenment through kindness, compassion and wisdom. This places meditation practice at the center of the healer's life and universe. Whether you are learning this path for personal interest or to become a professional, this is a path of clearing away the turmoil from within to free the self to live life in the way that best suits you. It is in the clearing of inner difficulties, past traumas and wrong beliefs that the healer's pathworking becomes the most difficult. This is sometimes called the path of the "wounded healer," as the wounds inflicted in daily life create compassion when faced in the dark and channeled through an open heart.

For this meditation, you will want to mentally prepare some prior to the session. This is more intensive than most meditations in this book and the reasoning is simple. If you really want to become a healer on your path, with the ability to intuitively know what to do for healing and alignment, you need to be very clear of mind and heart. This is the most powerful state for anyone that practices spirituality and magic, is true clarity of focus. Take a few minutes to let go of distracting thoughts and feelings before beginning. Perform deep breathing as often as you can, to keep a clearer state of mind for your healing practice. If you have a certain tool or method of healing that you use, you will want to keep it nearby for a focal point or contemplation during your meditation. Remember that any item such as flutes, drums, crystals, stones, herbs & oils, colors and many other items can be of aid to the healer that knows how to use them.

    Need: White, blue, or green candle
        Candleholder
        Sacred item or tool (crystals, etc.)
        Lighter or matches

Set up your altar space where you will not be disturbed for the meditation. If you have a meditation cushion or pillow to sit on, you may have it available as well. Place the candle of your choice in a candleholder in front of you, along with your chosen tool or sacred item and have a lighter or matches nearby. If you have many tools that you use for healing work, meditations can be done with them as you practice meditation over time. When you are ready, ignite the candle and take a few deep breaths to further clear your mind. Allow your gaze to soften as you see the candlelight, illuminating the room or area around you. When you feel that you are reaching a state of stillness and focus in your mind, bring your thoughts to this sacred tool or item that you have chosen for your meditation. Lift this sacred item and hold it in your hands or lap, allowing your mind to remain clear and focused. Let your mind direct you to all that is possible to be done with this sacred item in your hand. Consider the energy that it holds and projects into the world around it. Visualize the energy that flows through it, through you and into a person for healing ritual, or imagine the energy flowing out into the universe. See this energy in your mind in different colors or hear it as sounds from nature, such as waterfalls, crystalline tones, birds, wind in the trees, or whatever brings you to a peaceful place in your mind. Let this meditation be as a guide to finding your own inner peace to learn to channel healing energy and further your study and practice of healing. Practice this meditation for fifteen to twenty minutes, twice a day or as often as you can, while you walk the path of a healer. You may wish to keep notes in your journal of your meditations, feelings, sights and sounds that come about during the meditation session. When you are finished you may speak a short prayer to any deities or spirits and extinguish the candle.

Healer's Devotional Rite

Devotion to a healer's path is highly spiritual, difficult and rewarding. The healer that seeks to be a part of the healing process for many people must have an open heart and the ability to remain in that state most of their life. Healers will go through many challenges that require a powerful devotion beyond the mere words formed by human ideals. The healer needs to develop empathy to understand situations for others and have compassion for those that are lost within themselves and the world at large. It is a challenging path, while very spiritual, gentle and admirable on the surface. If you wish to devote yourself to the healer's path, even for a short period of time to heal yourself or to become your coven's healer, you will want to take your devotional rite very seriously. You may want to plan this rite with the new moon to begin a new path as a healer or perform it on the full moon to claim your place among the healing community.

Need: White, blue or green candle
Candleholder
Smudge wand (or loose herbs)
Smudge bowl

Bowl of fresh water
Pentacle disc
Crystal wand
Totem fetish item (if available)
Sacred item or tool for healing
Lighter or matches

Have space available that you will not be disturbed for the ritual You will want to dress lightly and go barefoot for the duration of the rite so plan accordingly. Begin by setting up the altar area in the center of your ritual space. Place the candle in the holder and put it on the pentacle disc with your fetish item in front of it. Place the bowl of fresh water to the left of the candle and the smudge wand and smudge bowl on the right. Depending on the size of your sacred item or tool, you may place it in front of the altar or set it on the altar beside the fetish. When your altar space is set up, ignite the smudge wand or loose herbs and stand in front of the altar. Take few deep breaths to clear your mind and focus on the ritual working. Holding the smudge wand or bowl with burning herbs in your projective hand, bend down and begin a cleansing on yourself as part of the devotional rite.

Holding the smudge near your feet, wave it gently back and forth and say...

"Blessed are my feet which carry me upon my path."

Let the smoke flow around your feet for a moment then move up to about your waist area. Wave the smudge gently back and forth again and say...

> *"Blessed are my loins which give me strength and creativity."*

Move to your belly after a moment and say...

> *"Blessed be my belly which gives me sustenance and life force."*

Move the smudge to your chest and waft the smoke around you saying...

> *"Blessed is my chest, which gives me strength, love and compassion."*

After a moment or two, move the smudge to your left hand and let the smoke flow over it then move to your right hand and speak the words over each...

> *"Blessed be my hands with which I interact with the world, giving and receiving. Let my hands flow with love and creativity."*

Now move the smudge near your lips...

> *"Blessed are my lips, with which I speak the truth and help to heal those that come to me."*

Now move the smudge to your forehead, in front of the third eye chakra and speak...

> *"Blessed are mine eyes, with which I see the many worlds. Let me see the many worlds with love and compassion as I walk the healer's path."*

Now you may place the smudge back upon the altar and ignite the candle on the pentacle disc and speak...

> *"By this sacred light I walk the Healer's path, to heal myself and any that come to me."*

Now lift the crystal wand and gently make a circle clockwise around the rim of the bowl of fresh water and speak...

> *"I cleanse and bless this sacred water, to aid me in my path as a healer. Let me become as clear and pure as the fresh waters of the Earth."*

Let yourself feel the water element flowing through you, clearing away the negative energy. Let yourself feel refreshed and then place the wand carefully back upon the altar. Lift your totem fetish and hold it before you in your receptive hand and speak...

> *"Sacred spirit, be as my guide on the Healer's path. Let me awaken my intuition and clear my thoughts, to hear you when you call my name. Grant me the power to transform with love and*

*light and to walk the Healer's path before me.
Hail Thee!"*

Now place the totem fetish back upon the altar and lift
your sacred tool for healing work. Hold this in your hands
in front of you, look to the sky and speak...

*"Spirits of the Earth and Sky, I call to thee to
aid me in this path as I walk forth as a Healer
among men. Let me learn much in the ways of
using this sacred (crystal, stone, etc.) Let me learn
the sacred ways of healing the spirit and the heart.
Grant me your blessing and guidance. Hail Thee!"*

You may sit now and meditate for a time over the
uses of this tool or item for healing work. If you wish,
you may perform the healer's meditation or spend time
to commune with your totems or guides or contemplate
your healing tools. Focus often on your heart chakra and
how you feel from within, to closely monitor your energy
for healing on this path.

Path of the Mystic

The path of the Mystic is a rarity in our modern era,
yet it encompasses and is the original purpose of many
religious traditions around the world. Long ago, the
Mystic was an advisor, seer, or astrologer that read and
understood the meanings of omens and celestial events,
as they pertained to the kingdom or land, the Mystic
resided in. Most often, our modern minds gravitate to

the ideas of Merlin and Morgan la Fey, Jesus, Buddha, a Zen master, spiritual gurus or many other religious figures throughout history. The Mystic is a figure found in the Tarot that may denote a Hermit as a spiritual seeker or a magician in its negative light, as a charlatan or "false prophet." The true meaning of the word, *mystic*, as defined by "Webster's New World Dictionary," is 1.) *of occult character or meaning*, and 2.) *one who professes to undergo mystical experiences by which he or she intuitively comprehends truths beyond human understanding."* This means that the mystic is a deeply religious and spiritual person that may be a member of any religion or religious practice, which seeks to gain an understanding of the cycle of life and death, the mysteries of the cosmos, etc. Therefore, the mystic may be a shaman, a witch, a practitioner of yoga and meditation, a Buddhist minister or priest, or even one of the Otherkin that has attained an enlightened understanding of the world through spiritual practices.

For the modern mystic, whether Otherkin, witch or shaman, this pathworking is one fraught with complexity and wisdom, power and spiritual freedom. The Mystic's path is closely akin to the Shapeshifter's pathworking, as the mystic must be well knowledged in many areas of life, love, death and magick. A Mystic may be a healer, a sage or wise man or woman, philosopher, a priest or priestess, teacher of occult arts, a witch, a shaman, alchemist or many other things at any given time. A Mystic's totems will incorporate spirits of wisdom and visionary power, both dark and light, such as the owl, snake, wolf, fox, crow, hawk and many others. The pathworking of the Mystic is one for the long-term practitioners of the occult arts and science, as it requires much diligence and wisdom to be true upon this path. It must remembered that the experiences of the Mystic are highly important and must be interpreted wisely for the Mystic to be successful on their path. These experiences are often described as *"transcendental,"* in modern terms and the practitioner must be given time to contemplate and fathom the meaning. An understanding of the mind, psychology, and spiritual teachings are a must for the true practitioner of the Mystic's path.

Most of modern witchcraft's tools originate from the time of the grimoire traditions, when alchemy and astrology were still in their infancy in Europe. Many of these tools, objects and artifacts are still very much a part of the mystic's pathworking. Sacred tools such as cauldrons, candles, glass bottles, crystal wands and many strange and obscure items will fill the home and shelves of the modern mystic, no matter their tradition. Some items such as the shaman's drum or rattles may also be incorporated in the Mystic's toolbox, if their tradition allows or desires its use.

While the Otherkin and modern witches are already a part of a *"mystical tradition,"* this does not make you an automatic mystic. It simply means that you are a part of the tradition, until you reach an "Elder status," or have the enlightening transcendent experiences you need to give you the wisdom to claim such a path or title. I never put much emphasis on attaining titles, as they can be just as degrading as uplifting to the individual. For the modern Mystic, claiming such a title may land you in the psychiatric ward, or make you the leader of a new cult in town. Neither of these truly fit the description of a real mystic, as it is in our ability to follow what we have learned by our experiences and develop what modern religions call, "*faith*," but I will term this as, "*sacred trust.*" Trust, especially *sacred trust*, is neither blind nor ignorant, but it does require a practice and following of the beliefs, rather than merely talking about them. A true modern Mystic can even follow the esoteric and spiritual teachings of the Christian bible and be quite effective, but it again requires practice and following the teachings, such as meditation and compassion.

Mystic's Meditation

The practice of meditation could be the main focus of many modern mystical traditions. Meditation, when practiced regularly and effectively, will grant the practitioner many deeply spiritual experiences, after all of the human traumas and dramas have been healed and understood. It is in reaching past the difficulties of life and emotions that the mystic learns to excel in their field of expertise. This is where the true experiences begin to happen, which is why I stated that the mystic must be diligent on the path and be capable of understanding and interpreting what is being experienced. Journeying in consciousness beyond ordinary reality is just a pipe dream for the common person that wallows in the shallow end of life. It is in the experience of transcending the flesh of life and death that we realize that we are the consciousness that continues after death of the body; the experience of the immortal soul, that creates a newborn Mystic. It could be said that this path emphasizes experience and the seeking of experience for the sake of knowledge, wisdom and power.

For this meditation, you will want to find an image of space or some cosmic events, whether real or imaginary. This type of imagery can help us to get out of our normal minds and reach into the esoteric and celestial aspects of life and death. If you wish, you may gather a few items before beginning.

Need: White, black or blue candle
   Incense for wisdom
       (frankincense, sage, mugwort, etc.)
   Bells or singing bowls (celestial sounds)
   Space or cosmic imagery
   Lighter or matches

To begin, set up your meditation space with the candle in front of you and incense in a holder beside of the candle. If you have singing bowls or bells that are pleasant sounding, or even a recording of them, you may have it available for an aid. Place your image of the cosmos or deep space before you to give your mind a visual image to work with. Spend a few minutes prior to the meditation to study this image. When you are ready, light the candle and incense and ring the bell or bowl with a striker, or start the pre-recorded music. Begin to take several deep slow breaths, allowing your lungs to completely fill and empty during the breathing. This will push more fresh oxygenated blood to your brain waking it up and giving you a boost of consciousness. Now, listen to the sound of the bell, ringing it yourself if you need to and allow your breathing to return to normal. Clear your mind of all thought, and create a visual image of your self, where you are now, seated in meditation. Now let your mental image begin to grow, through the ceiling of your room or space, bigger than the house you live in, and continuing to grow until you are as big as the earth, seated and looking into deep space. Let your image continue to grow until you leave the Earth and begin to see into vast reaches of space. Now listen closely as you may begin to hear sounds coming from space. Allow yourself to listen to view the wonders of the universe for a short time.

When you are ready, slowly bring your visualization back down to size, by allowing yourself to shrink, back down to the earth's size then smaller and smaller until you are back to your house and sitting in your room again. Settle yourself and your consciousness back within your body, before opening your eyes to finish the meditation. When you are back to normal and ready, you may extinguish the candle.

Visualization practices like this one, can aid in expanding the mind beyond the sense of self that we get stuck in. Breathing practices and meditation with sounds playing or heard during the process, will have a profound effect upon the mind of the practitioner, aiding them in transcending the body and typical mind frame common in humanity today. Practice this meditation often and you will see results and eventually be able to interact more consciously with the visualization. You may also use a drum for shamanic work with this meditation practice as well.

Mystic's Devotional Rite

As the mystic is just as spiritual as magical in many traditions, so is the rite of devotion to this pathworking. Mystics have long been the keepers of strange and rare objects as well as spiritual teachers and guides, so if you have any special items such as crystals, oils, herbs, roots, bones, etc., that you would like incorporate into this rite, by all means do so.

Need: Totem fetish
    (hawk, owl or crow feathers are suggested)
    Black or white candle & holder
    Smudge bowl & charcoal blocks
    Resin incense such as copal, dragon's blood, frankincense, myrrh, etc
    Septagram disc
    Lighter or matches

Set up your altar with the black or white candle in a holder, resting on the septagram disc. Place the smudge bowl to the left of the candle with a charcoal block placed within it. Your totem fetish item can be placed in front of the candle, along with any other items you wish to make a part of this ritual. To begin ignite the candle and charcoal block and let the charcoal really start to burn before pouring any incense upon it. (Some resins will put out charcoal when they melt, so you may need to fan it to keep it burning for a few minutes.) Once you have the incense burning. Waft the smoke over you and clear your mind, focusing on your path. Waft the smoke again over you and speak...

> *"By the sacred light, I seek the path of the Mystic, to walk with wisdom and power in life and beyond. By the spirits of the four directions, above and below, I dedicate my spirit unto this path of knowledge. Guide me in seeing in new ways, of the life in the world around me and beyond. Hear me and hail thee!"*

Now lift your totem fetish item from the altar and hold it close to your third eye between your eyebrows. Be silent for moment then speak...

> *"Sacred spirits of life and wisdom, let me attain the visionary sight I seek, to walk upon this path with knowledge. Guide me as I seek a vision from within my life and consciousness, to dedicate and devote my spirit, mind and body. Hail thee!"*

Sitting before the altar, hold the feather or totem fetish and any other small items such as an amethyst crystal in your hand, and begin a rapid deep breathing.

Clear your mind and reach as deeply into meditation as you can, without forcing any mental image. Clear your mind of images or distractions while performing the deep breathing and allow the vision to come to you in time during this meditation. This is intended to help you achieve a subtle transcendent state to reach into for guidance and knowledge when you need it. You may eventually see images that upset you or that spark a certain feeling that you cannot shake off. This is the spirit's way of giving you a sense of purpose, to pursue until you achieve your goal and move into something new. If you wish to perform shamanic journey with this ritual, it can aid you in finding your inner vision of a mystical path to follow.

The Mystic's pathworking is about visionary experiences and following the teachings that you receive in meditation and shamanic journeys, omens and dreams. Be thoughtful and contemplate what you see and find in the many worlds, and you will find wisdom in the strangest of places.

Trickster – Path to the Crossroads

The last, but certainly not the least archetypal pathworking, is that of the Trickster, Spirit of the Crossroads. This figure is prominent in lore and legend, especially where there is darkness or evil afoot. The trickster is not the embodiment of evil or malice, contrary to much popular belief, but a figure that understands the old must be destroyed in order for the new to arise. The Trickster is highly misunderstood due to its ability to destroy without hesitation or fear, as the wise trickster knows that this will bring about something better in time. The Trickster is also a master of the path or road we walk in life and can be called upon at the crossroads where we stop to consider our next move. Crossroads are places of making decisions, removing blocks or changing our direction, as well as a place of destruction of the old things we carry as baggage. The trickster can help us to make the proper decisions to transform our life if we but trust in his "evil grin."

The Trickster is an archetype from many traditions all over the globe. He may be as Loki, from the Norse tradition that through his many tricks and lies, eventually brought about the destiny of the gods. The Trickster appears as the coyote or fox of Native American traditions that stole fire among other things for mankind. The Trickster may be as Papa Legba, a central figure of New Orleans and Haitian voodoo and hoodoo traditions. In Afro-Brazilian traditions, he is Exu, or Eshu Ellegbara, master of the roads, healer and provider of opportunities and fortune. In classical traditions, he is Puck, or Robin Goodfellow, the merry prankster that causes havoc to bring about change. The Christian "devil" may also be considered a Trickster spirit that grants abilities and changes to those that call upon him. A Trickster is not necessarily the anti-god, nor anti-good, but the Yin to their Yang or the equal and opposite spirit of balance and harmony. It is our loss of understanding in balance and the need for darkness that we judge the Trickster in a negative light or as an evil spirit or deity.

Many Trickster spirits of the crossroads are also connected with the cemetery and the realms of the dead. A crossroads in many ancient traditions was understood not only as a place where two paths meet, but also as a place at the gates between life and death. Many of these trickster spirits stand at the gates and serve as psychopomps, guiding the dead into the next realm. This connects the Trickster with shamanic practices as the shaman was sometimes thought of as a Trickster that taught lessons as well as guiding dead souls and performing healing. Tricksters are a complex lot that may serve to guide us and open the road for us in life as well as taking us to the realm of death.

For witches and Otherkin considering this complex pathworking, to align the spiritual self with the Trickster archetype may bring about a lot more changes within your life and spirit than you expect. The Trickster is a free spirit, and may lead you to finding your own inner and outer freedom in time. The Trickster is very powerful no matter how he, or sometimes she, manifests. Your results will be your own. If approached with a clear and focused mind, your life may change forever for the better. But if approached with fear or malice, you may find yourself in places you never wanted to be. The road and decisions are yours.

Contacting and aligning our spiritual path with the Trickster will require much in the way of deeper thought and courage. Totems of this path, just as any, should be given utmost respect and consideration when working with bones, claws, teeth, etc. I say this because one of the most popular Trickster totems is the coyote, which in many areas of the country, is a hated animal and often killed for sport. I would not advise any ill will towards any totems of the trickster, if you were to align successfully with it. Coyote magic can be tricky to work with as well, due to its very nature. The coyote's magic may or may not work or appear effective, yet it has a tendency to turn out for the better in the long run. Other totems of this archetype will include hyenas, jackals, foxes, crows and ravens, weasels, donkeys and even at times, rabbits.

The Trickster is often depicted as a shapeshifter but as I said earlier in this chapter, the energy is a little different. The Trickster's energy is fun loving and enjoys a good joke or prank, often at the expense of others. The Trickster may be an accomplished magician, living as an occultist that adapts to the changing needs of life, while the shapeshifter must shift its shape to adapt and survive. This may be better compared between a classic werewolf in legend and movies, hiding what he knows he did by being quiet and going about his work, and the eccentric old man or Voodoo priest, that runs an occult shop in New Orleans, having fun with all the people that enter while selling his wears. These two would not be the same in any room together and are undeniably different in their energy and way of life.

Trickster Meditation

While meditation and a Trickster archetype may not appear to go together, meditation is highly necessary on this strange path. If we try to become as the Trickster archetype, without understanding the wisdom required to achieve it, we end up just being ridiculous and /or annoying. It is the wisdom of knowing the difference between when the spirit or the ego guides us that determines the Trickster's effectiveness. We also must not be connected to outcomes, as the people involved in these "tricks," still make their own decisions. It is very difficult to place the proper energy into a situation to make changes and be for sure of the outcome. This requires one to be in a very deep state of mind and spiritual alignment to understand a situation among people and achieve success. Also the success of the trickster's magic may take time, even years to come to the original goal, depending upon the people involved and their choices along the way.

When aligning one's spiritual path with the Trickster archetype, you may wish to use dark or devilish humor in your altar imagery to inspire you during the meditation. This does not have to be "evil imagery," just a dark sense of humor to bring about the spirit's attention and aid. Devil figure candles or statues or images of a skull with a top hat may be present to aid you in your alignment. Purple and/or black candles and tobacco or wormwood as incense may also be a favorite, on the altar of the Otherkin aligned with the Trickster spirit.

For this meditation, you may choose whether or not to use your altar and candles, incense, etc, but these may help you in difficult situations. The important part is your focus and inner understanding of the Trickster's path. Be seated in a place where you will not be disturbed and allow plenty of time for the meditation, without being distracted. Begin with deep breathing practice to bring yourself into a meditative state and clear your mind of all thoughts and emotions. Remember that after you get a little light-headed or dizzy, let your breathing return to normal and begin to count your breathing cycles from one to ten and then repeat. When your mind is clear and focused, begin to think about a time when something you experienced seemed to be wrong or to turn out badly. This is a time when you or someone around you got hurt, whether emotionally or physically and the whole situation was deemed "bad." Now consider what happened before and after this experience or situation, set your mind on finding the "good," that eventually occurred because of this negative situation. This is an act of the Trickster spirit, to cause something to go "wrong," that leads to something better. Understanding how things change and are determined by our own choices and abilities is a part of what the Trickster spirit does. Meditate on this type of situation or experiences and ask the Trickster spirit of your choice to help you to understand their ways and how to see from a broader view of the situation. When you are finished with this meditation, give thanks to the spirit that guides you and keep notes in your journal for information later about the workings of the Trickster spirits in your life. Practice often.

Trickster Devotional Rite

This devotion is based in the traditional ways of contacting the Trickster or spirit of the crossroads. If you wish to devote yourself to this pathworking, you will need to find a crossroads that you can go to late at night or early in the morning before sunrise. You may incorporate this into your full moon ritual at some time or whenever the energy feels right for you to perform this devotion. A traditional crossroads is a four-way intersection that carries on for eight blocks in all directions, but information exists about three-way and other forms of the crossroads and their uses. This may mean getting away from the city to find long roads in the country or being near the center of the city or town you live in. Consider the places that the roads are longest from an intersection and count the blocks away from it in all directions. If there is a particular tool you wish to work with or something that you wish to learn more about, take this with you to the crossroads near midnight. This may be candles or a wand to represent magical work, a musical instrument, etc. Take this tool with you and be at the crossroads at midnight.

You may want to bring an offering with you such as tobacco, a cigar or rum or you may offer your self and devotion to the spirits, the choice is yours. Stand at the crossroads when there is no traffic coming and hold this item into the air, looking into the night sky or the moon and speak...

"Spirits of the Crossroads, I seek to devote myself to your ways. Guide me in learning the ways and powers of the Crossroads. Let me see your blessings in my life with understanding and wisdom. Guide me in using this tool of power

for my own benefit and for the benefit of those that come to me. I devote myself to thee! I Devote Myself to thee! I seek the path of the Crossroads spirits! I walk in the ways of the Trickster! Hail Thee!!

Remain at the Crossroads until after midnight or until the sun rises, contemplating this item that you have brought and want to learn to use in your life. Be sincere and honest about your intentions and you may reap the benefits of working with the spirits of the Crossroads, and learning the ways of the Trickster archetype.

Chapter Sixteen
Becoming as the Moon

After we have followed the moon for a number of years and learned and experienced much under her influence, we will begin to see ourselves changing in our views and ideals, to emulate or integrate what we have experienced. This is the process of becoming as the Moon, to shine a light into the darkness of life and find the magick that naturally calls to us. The moon holds many mysteries as it journeys across the night sky and we will learn much if we pay close attention to her journeys and compare them to our own. This is the other side of the Otherkin experience; attaining an enlightened view of life and the world and carrying it out in our own way, to live the life we were meant for. The ways of the Moon are many and both of the light and the darkness. It is in darkness that we create then bring forth our creations into the light of day. It is in darkness that we rest and heal ourselves so that we have the strength and wisdom to continue on our paths. It is also the darkness that challenges us, to face our fears and learn things we may not have thought we needed in life. These are all ways in which the Moon holds influence upon us, and if we are diligent and take our time to learn rather than running from our troubles, we will find much wisdom to become as a guide to others that are beginning their journeys into the darkness of life and the self. Shamanic and other magical and spiritual teachings need to make a return to the forefront of life, being incorporated into schools and families, as well as churches and businesses. These teachings give us and others, an understanding of life from the spiritual perspective, helping us to understand why we experience certain things, feelings, desires, and how to cope with them or integrate them into our being to become whole as the full moon herself. It is by the Moon that we reflect the light of the sun onto others that are in trouble in their journeys in life and need assistance in understanding what they feel and why and how to return to a better state of being. But if we are to help others, we must understand our path and imitate the ways of the Moon.

Understanding & Imitating the Ways

Following and becoming as the Moon in the modern world is not easy, as many of us work jobs or have families, which do not allow us to be awake with the moon at night contemplating deeper topics and working magick. Not that it only requires being awake when the moon is up, but the need is to spend time under the moon in rituals such as, *"Calling Down the Moon,"* or other rites to more completely align the spirit with her sacred mysteries. If we do not seek the mysteries in life, we will not likely find them. But just as the Zen tradition states, *"we must seek without seeking,"* meaning we must spend time going within our self in meditation and shamanic journey to find and understand what we truly seek in life. There is an amount of information that we receive from the outside world but the rest must come from within us. This is the process of following our instincts, intuition, desires, and visions of life and our future.

If you truly wish to become as the Moon, you can work with this rite of calling her down on your own, to find information and guidance on your path, through the darkness of life and the night. Traditionally, this ritual is intended for the full moon, but we can always use our inner vision to work with her when we need it. Be seated in meditation, and you may light white or silver candles and burn an incense such as sandalwood, myrrh, willow, jasmine, or any herbs or fragrances that align with the lunar current of energy. When you are ready, begin to breathe deeply and clear your mind of all thoughts and emotions. Focus on turning your attention inward to speak to the Moon Goddess or a lunar spirit that you work with. Call their name three times and imagine yourself sitting on a beach or near a natural body of water. Let this scene fill in around you and let go of where you "physically" are located. See the moon in this vision rising slowly in the distance and growing brighter than ever before. This scene will become very surreal in your mind as the lunar spirit or Moon Mother shines her light over you and your surroundings, and begins to speak to you. Listen carefully to what she has to say and ask her your questions, tell her your concerns, whatever you need to say or do in this vision. Spend some time in conversation and listening to what she has to say, then give her thanks with great sincerity and bid her farewell. If your vision allows, you may reach up to hug or embrace her, as the moon in this place can be the same size as you. This sacred embrace of the Moon is a highly enlightening and thrilling experience that will leave you feeling many new feelings of love and joy and grant you a new understanding of your spirituality and abilities as a practitioner of magick. After this sacred embrace, give her thanks again and slowly allow yourself to return to normal consciousness and open your eyes; fully returning to the room or place your physical body is located. Remember what this spirit said to you and apply it to your life and concerns. You may come back from this meditation with the feeling of things being ok or like it is going to turn out and everything will be alright. You can go into this meditation anytime you are in need and this will help you to align yourself more fully with the powers of the lunar current, and eventually become as the Moon.

Being as a Beacon of Wisdom

Attaining wisdom on this path can be one of the most difficult things to accomplish. First there is always the argument of, "what is wisdom?" This can be debated and argued for decades among people and never reach a full agreement. True wisdom may come from many sources, with some that might surprise you. The obvious places are various ancient religious texts, which tend to be considered stupid, trivial, or useless by many ignorant modern people. This horrible consideration of ancient knowledge is because of the ways in which it was paradoxically written, to be figured out by others rather than explaining things away. It also requires us to experience the same or a similar circumstance that these ancient people experienced, to reach the revelation of understanding.

The most surprising places to find wisdom are in nature and within your self. Nature has a way of giving us a glimpse of things from beyond without making a big fuss over it, as it is a part of the natural order of things. Attaining wisdom from nature requires us to be more receptive and open to that wisdom which surrounds us daily but is rarely ever seen or acknowledged. This same wisdom is translated often to our birth language when we go within the inner worlds of meditation, dreamscapes and shamanic journey and can be spoken to us by our guides, spirits, gods, or daemons, in that realm. This is a long process in attaining wisdom that many people won't have the perseverance to continue. It takes many years to reach a point of wisdom and understanding in life and the world and their will always be someone that creates doubt about the understanding or wisdom of an individual. This is why the "age of the guru," in the 1960's and 70's ended rather abruptly.

In being as a beacon of wisdom, we must learn many things and un-learn many more. Attaining the ability to go within at a moments notice to reach for an answer to daily problems or struggles in the world, takes much ability in self-discipline and the practice of meditation. Practicing non-attachment, to keep a clear mind and focus is one of the major keys to finding that wisdom and ability in this lifetime. This is not easy as we tend to be attached to the world we live in and each of us have our issues with being in control of situations, differing opinions, concerns, fears, etc, that cloud our judgment and keep us from the spiritual attainment and the understanding that is naturally within us.

So how does one create a practice of becoming more wise and true to the spirit within on this path of the moon? It is by continually returning to clarity in meditation, along with using common sense and practical knowledge when it comes to others and life in the world, that we find the wisdom we seek. We cannot save people from their problems, if they don't want or refuse our help. We can't save people from their own lessons, and it is up to them to answer the questions, or repeat the lesson at a later time. While this sounds cruel to many people, this is the way and wisdom of the moon. As I stated earlier, attaining wisdom isn't easy. While I make no claims at being some wise guru, or monk from the mountains, I want to encourage the next generation of witches and Otherkin to reach for wisdom no matter what your position or career in this life. The more of us that begin to use the wisdom of the Moon and spirit, the more it may catch on in society and eventually make a better world for all of us to live in. The greatest thing about walking a path of wisdom is that eventually it allows you to follow your own cycles.

Following Your Own Cycles

Whether we realize it or not, we often tend to follow the cycles of other people and things that may not be of true benefit to us. We have all had a time when we didn't know what to do with our lives, or tried something new that didn't work out, and it is in the realization that it isn't working that is important. I have been stuck in cycles like this before as well and want to encourage more people to see what is happening around them and in their lives. It can require us to see from a larger perspective of life to understand this and how we get stuck in these cycles. When we get stuck in a cycle that really isn't productive for us, whether spiritually or physically, our lives will tend to have little to no meaning or purpose. We just keep turning the wheel, as if it will turn out different on the next rotation. Many people in the world today are taught to just get some job and stay with it, and bosses and managers use fear to control those that disagree with rules and regulations, no matter how ludicrous those rules are. We are taught and sometimes forced to put up with things and situations that are detrimental and even destructive to our life and well being as well as the society as a whole. This is how modern society and our world have grown so damaged and out of balance. The more of our population that has agreed to be enslaved by these rules and regulations out of fear of job loss or retaliation, the more of these rules and regulations have been applied to push people down. This keeps us from being whole and healthy, mentally, emotionally, spiritually, and physically.

In parts of the country where more people are standing up for themselves and stand together against wrongful laws or rules, such as with the "Occupy" movement, the more our world will be changed forever. This is the ability and choice of these people to follow there own cycles, whether as a larger group, or as individuals, and stand up for what they know to be right. This is a part of the process of claiming our ability to follow our own cycles, making our own rules and living by them. These may come in different ways and at different times for each of us, but if we answer that inner calling, we claim and follow our own cycle in life. We can all achieve this in our lives, whether on a smaller scale such as starting our own business or writing a book, or on a much grander scale of making changes to the process and fairness of laws or changing the way businesses treat and deal with people. This process of freeing ourselves from the cycles of others isn't easy, but well worth it if we can achieve it. The witch of ancient times didn't stand for rules and regulations that intended to enslave her or him, and neither should we in the modern era. Follow your own cycles every chance you get in life, and find the freedom that will naturally follow.

Afterward – My Experiences

I have often wondered about the experiences of other authors, when I was reading their books and learning on my path. With a book and topics that work through an entire year of seasonal and magical information, I feel it necessary to let you see how I have broken down the months and understand them to be in process in my life. I can't say that you will have the same results, but I can let you see through my eyes, so to speak. So, in this section, I invite to read about my own experiences in working through the "wheel of the year" with a magical perspective and following the moon.

This book began its conception in mid-December of 2013, under the Oak Moon's wisdom and guidance. I was still awaiting return on the copyright on my first book, when the ideas started coming to me. So I simply looked online to see what I could find. A short search granted me the names of the lunar months and I jotted them down in my notebook and pondered on the topic for a while. By January, under the Wolf Moon, the topics grew into notes and ideas for rites and workings, as I was first publishing, *"The Book of Satyr Magick,"* on Lulu.com for the first time. So at this time, book 1 and 2 are growing roots in different ways. As February and the Storm Moon came along, I found myself clearing away the lasting remnants of a bad relationship, that kept dragging on. Since the Storm Moon was on Valentine's Day in 2014, it doubled the energy for the working and allowed me to remove the last feelings and gain a greater understanding of the why's and how's of the relationship. I am glad to say I've been free from it since, with no lasting negative side effects nor ill-wishing upon her. So late February and early March comes along and I have a disaster of a break-in occur at some property I own, which sets me back for a while. Remember that February is for strengthening our roots before emergence in spring. I took the time off from writing for a couple weeks as the early spring came in and while showing minor signs of growth and encouragement, I didn't accomplish much. Finally I cleared this away, just in time for the Chaste Moon of March in which I went to the crossroads for justice and protection of my property. I also grew frustrated with publishing issues and decided to hire my current publisher, which has went well, thus far. By April, the Seed Moon and time for planting, I really hit writing hard again, trying to accomplish as much in each day as possible. There were other subtle signs of the season showing them selves as well. Since spring often means love is in the air, I performed my first wedding as a minister on the 19th of the month and received some good feedback from guests and the couple alike. I was pretty busy during April and pushed as much as I could for growth and development of my dreams while the season was allowing me, too. The Hare Moon of May rolled in to see another couple asking me to perform their wedding when they set a date for it, as well as more writing on this book. May is a time of freeing your wild nature and celebrating life, and within certain circumstances, I definitely have. Earlier in the month, I found myself with more topics in mind for later books and began my research into them to break ground, begin working the rituals and take notes. I have in the last week, began helping a rather high-profile client, with some troubles they are having and trying to help them adjust to the changes that have occurred in their life.

Now as I am writing this, it is May 27th of 2014, and my second book is nearly complete and ready to send to the publisher, to start over again. By June and the Dyad Moon, the old has made way for the new and I will be starting other projects such as a paganspace page and possibly an online store, to further this career. Remember that June is the recognition of the duality or "other" nature within us all, and I may have other strange things coming along with it that I hope will prove fruitful. It will be August or September of this year before I begin to see any proceeds from my efforts now, and I hope that I will have a fruitful harvest in autumn that continues to grow into a new future for my children and myself.

So there you have it. I know that this isn't much but it gives you a perspective of what I'm experiencing while working and walking this path. It is in the understanding and application of the knowledge and looking at the subtleties that we learn to see things from an older, more ancient point of view. I hope that you enjoy this book as much as I have enjoyed writing it. Thank you and look for more of my work, coming later.

May 2014
Lotuswulf Satyrhorn

Bibliography and Suggested Reading

Satyrhorn, Lotuswulf *The Book of Satyr Magick:*
Otherkin Shamanic Sorcery
Bloomington, In. AuthorHouse 2014

Alvarado, Denise *The Voodoo Hoodoo Spellbook*
Creole Moon 2009 pdf edition

Andrews, Ted *Animal Speak* St. Paul, Minn.
Llewellyn 2001
Animal Wise Jackson, Tenn.
Dragonhawk Publishing 1999

Belanger, Michelle *The Dictionary of Demons-*
Names of the Damned, Llewellyn 2012
The Vampire Ritual Book 2004, pdf edition

Connolly, S. *Daemonolater's Guide to Daemonic Magick*
Co. DB Publishing 2009
The Complete Book of Daemonolatry
Co. DB Publishing 2006

D'Emerys, Strix *realmagick.com*
"What are the names of the thirteen moons of the
year?" Online article 2011

Dewr, Dagonet *Sacred Paths for Modern Men- a wake up call from your twelve archetypes*
    St. Paul, Minn. Llewellyn 2007

Cunningham, Scott *Wicca- a Guide for the Solitary Practitioner* St. Paul Minn. Llewellyn 2004
    Cunningham's Encyclopedia of Magical Herbs
    St. Paul Minn. Llewellyn 2008

Rosean, Lexa *The Encyclopedia of Magical Ingredients- a Wiccan Guide to Spellcasting*
    Paraview Pocket Books, NY 2005

Illes, Judika *The Element Encyclopedia of Witchcraft*
    HarperElement London 2005
    The Encyclopedia of Spirits
    HarperOne NY 2009

Grimassi, Raven *The Witch's Familiar- Spiritual Partnerships for Successful Magic*
    Woodbury, Minn. Llewellyn 2003

Klens-Bigman, Deborah and Raymond A. Sosnowski *The Way of the Bow- the Kyudo path to a disciplined mind*
Sweetwater Press 2008

Wauters, Ambika *Chakras and their Archetypes- Uniting Energy Awareness and Spiritual Growth*
    Crossing Press, Berkeley 1997

Summers, Montague *The Werewolf in Lore and Legend*
Dover Publications, NY 2003

Galenorn, Yasmine *Embracing the Moon*
St. Paul Minn. Llewellyn 1998

Yamakage, Motohisa *The Essence of Shinto- Japan's Spiritual Heart* Kodansha Intl. 2006